The

CRAFT *of the*
CLASSROOM

A SURVIVAL GUIDE

THIRD EDITION

LEARNING RESOURCES CENTRE
Havering College
of Further and Higher Education

MICHAEL MARLAND
CBE MA FRSA FCP HonDEd HonDUniv

Honorary Fellow, Institute of Education
London University

Heineman

D1382384

371·102

15025

Heinemann Educational Publishers
Halley Court, Jordan Hill, Oxford, OX2 8EJ
a division of Harcourt Education Ltd.
Heinemann is a registered trademark of Harcourt Education Ltd.

OXFORD MELBOURNE AUCKLAND
JOHANNESBURG BLANTYRE GABORONE
IBADAN PORTSMOUTH NH (USA) CHICAGO

British Library Cataloguing in Publication Data
A catalogue record for this book is available from the British Library

ISBN 0 435 80609 2

Author photograph by Catherine Shakespeare Lane

Designed and typeset by J & L Composition, Filey, North Yorkshire
Printed and bound in Great Britain by Biddles Ltd, Guildford

Tel: 01865 888058 www.heinemann.co.uk

Contents

About the author

Michael Marland is one of the country's most popular educational authors. After experience as Head of English and Director of Studies in comprehensive schools, he was a leading Headteacher for thirty years. After ten years as Head of Woodberry Down School, he founded North Westminster Community School, a school with a range of specialisms, which he led for twenty years.

Now retired from actual school leadership, he is extensively involved in the professional development of classroom management, curriculum planning, the arts, inter-cultural education, pastoral care, and working with parents. He is General Editor of the Heinemann School Management Series. His recent books include *Managing the Arts in the Curriculum* and *The Secondary School Tutor's Role*. His publications have gained him a Fellowship of the College of Teachers, and he has Honorary Doctorates from Kingston University and the University of Surrey at Roehampton, as well as an Honorary Fellowship from the Institute of Education at London University.

Preface

Classroom management is at the heart of school teaching, and *The Craft of the Classroom* was specially planned to assist the professional development of secondary-school teachers. It has been widely read and used by very many indeed to improve their practice further. This new edition has been substantially revised in the light of secondary school teaching needs for the twenty-first century. Many readers will be experienced teachers, taking the opportunity to review and extend their work as part of their Continuous Professional Development. Very many readers will be Newly Qualified Teachers or those still in training. Therefore, the text fully takes into account the statutory *Professional Standards for Qualified Teachers*[1], which came into force in September 2002, and which have to be met by the end of the Induction year. The recently-established Induction process for Newly Qualified Teachers is one of the major developments in British education, and places an appropriate emphasis on 'Teaching and Class Management' (Section 3.3 of the statutory summary)[1]. This edition is designed to complement that sequence, and further to enrich the provision for newly-qualified teachers, which has now been researched as being praised and 'enjoyed' by most teachers[2].

The focus is on 'Teaching and Class Management' for all secondary positions. Subject knowledge and pastoral care are not specifically included, but the class management focus of the revised book also includes the statutory requirements of 'Professional Values and Practice' and 'Knowledge and Understanding'. Also, the aspects of classroom management are related to the Key Stage Three strategy, ICT, literacy across the curriculum, and Citizenship. Similarly, there has been a detailed review of changes in school procedures, equipment, and overall whole-school curriculum planning.

Acknowledgements

I, of course, take responsibility for any errors of fact or omissions. I should, however, very much like to thank the many people who advised me, including those experienced teachers who had used the first or second editions in their own training and later in their support of their team members, and many teachers in training or in their early years. For detailed written analysis I am grateful to David Howe and H. Walker. I should especially like to thank David Lambert, who was at the time of my preparing this revision leading the Master of Teaching degree at the Institute of Education at London University, and who gave me detailed and very helpful advice, both at an early stage and on a later draft.

Michael Marland

Abbreviations used in the text

CEP Career Entry Profile
DfEE Department for Education and Employment (now the Department for Education and Skills (DfES))
D&T Design & Technology
EAL English as an Additional Language
GTC General Teaching Council
ICT Information Communication Technology
IEP Individual Education Plan
ITT Initial Teacher Training
LEA Local Education Authority
NQT Newly Qualified Teacher
OHP Overhead Projector
PRT Post-Registration Truancy
PSHE Personal, Social and Health Education
QCA Qualifications and Curriculum Authority
QTS Qualified Teacher Status
SATs Standard Assessment Tests
SEN Special Educational Needs
TTA Teacher Training Agency

1

Starting points

The core of secondary school education is what happens day in and day out in the ordinary classrooms. Whatever legislation may demand, whatever beyond-timetable activity may flourish, or whatever support there may be, it is in the classroom interchange of teacher and taught that a pupil's success or failure is gained. The major changes of recent decades have brought different organization of responsibility for the work of schools, changes in modes of curriculum planning, more extensive testing, sharply increased accountability, and a greater interchange with the communities outside the school, but the centre of the work of the school is still the classroom.

It is almost platitudinous to say it all depends on the teacher. True, but what does that actually mean? What is the essence of the quality of teaching? The more you look at schooling in practice, the more you study research and observation, and the more you consider the real problems of helping young people learn, the more you are forced to the simple conclusion that the work of individual teachers is the most important factor. This was strongly put by the central government 'Board of Education' as long ago as 1937 in a pithy statement that is still just as true: 'The success of a school depends in the long run on the personal influence of its teachers.'[3]

The whole-school organization, curriculum planning, environment, leadership, and ethos are certainly necessary considerations for good schooling, but they are not sufficient. Indeed, the greatest test of them is the extent to which they enable or hinder the individual teacher to work better. For instance, excellent teaching can be inhibited if there is not a coherent curriculum plan into which it can fit.

1

The key to success

Yet the success of the individual teacher depends on more than impressive personality and specialized knowledge. Whatever her subject or whatever teaching method he is adopting, the teacher is primarily working with a group of young people: the individuals cannot be helped if the teacher cannot successfully manage the group as a whole. There is a craft of managing the group in a secondary school classroom that is vital for the pupils. Every teacher must be proficient in this craft. The encouraging thing is that it can be learnt, practised, and improved. It is not merely 'natural', and when it has been acquired you and your pupils will collaborate more profitably and enjoy your time together in school more. Greater success with managing the *group* allows you to be the better able to help the *individual*.

For many years schools have been in the forefront of political controversy. Many people have publicly criticized schools and teachers and there continues, and will continue to be, fierce debate about many schooling matters. As public arguments swirl around different aspects of schooling, it is important to keep the classroom as the key centre for education and to highlight the central art of the teacher as managing that classroom.

This substantially revised book is an attempt to re-emphasize the classroom as the centre of secondary educational focus and to describe the elements of the craft of its management in a way that can be used for self-observation, analysis, mutual support, and development.

The emphasis on classroom skills

In many ways secondary schools have advanced in the last few decades. Some of the legislative and advisory steps taken by central government tend to be narrowly and mechanically interpreted if the staff in a school do not read the full text (for example, the overall introduction to the National Curriculum[4]), which often has more flexibility than is quoted in hurried staffroom exchanges. For instance, the National Literacy and Numeracy strategies encourage this incorporation of knowledge and skills in every subject course.

One of the greatest changes has been a much increased attention to the details of classroom teaching. This, valuably, has exponentially increased teacher-to-teacher classroom observation. Interesting and important studies of what actually goes on between teacher and pupils have been a mine for the student of classroom technique. (The most helpful are listed in the reading list on p. 144.) Anti-racist and gender-equality studies have focused on the fascinating details of the different ways in which teachers organize, speak to, react to, and set assignments for pupils. Even so, the craft of teaching had been less thoroughly scrutinized than it deserves, but there is now a diverse collection of detailed observation from which to learn.

By the first decade of the twenty-first century, schools had developed far more detailed, active, and positive ways of inducting new teachers, monitoring their actual classroom work, and supporting its development. This is part of the 'Performance Management' for which every school has to have a formal policy. The term 'appraisal' is used by the DfEE as 'synonymous with "performance management"' (as confirmed in the 2000 *Performance Management in Schools*[5]). However, it is also used more widely. Whereas 'Performance Management' centres round an annual review cycle, the mutual and team-leader observation of classroom practice can be prompted by a variety of interests – and requested by a teacher: 'Could you find time to observe me handling my new use of improvization in PSHE lessons? I'd really value your views.' What is so often helpful is that the fresh eye both finds aspects to praise which the observed teacher has taken for granted, and notices a small point or two which need reconsideration. It is possible occasionally to have an odd way of putting things, a way of standing, or a way of relating to that pupil which you have not realized and which are easily adjusted. Observation really helps.

The emphasis of initial training on in-school experience has been associated with an admirable growth in the importance of 'induction'. It is difficult sometimes for busy senior teachers to develop the precise skills of teaching classroom management, but most schools offer a good programme. Similarly, newly qualified teachers should be able to draw upon specific support in their schools from their Induction Tutor and Head of Department (who may be the Induction Tutor). This aspect of a school's responsibilities needs continuous review and development. Whilst the Induction Tutor of a newly qualified teacher needs to cover a wide range of professional concerns, from curriculum planning to home–school relationships, 'the craft of the classroom' is the heart of it.

My book has been very widely used for many years by both student teachers and those in the early years of their teaching, and I have been told very often how helpful they have found it. This third edition grows from the core of the original book. The developments relate especially to our even higher ambitions of inclusiveness for all and the challenges of the twenty-first century. Recent research into classroom practice has been incorporated. All aspects of the classroom and inter-personal aspects of the government's requirements for QTS are included. It is important that these demands are used positively, and flexible and imaginative use made of them. Further, as a NQT, the Induction Tutor in your school will be able to support you more effectively the more thoroughly you have considered classroom management. I hope that you will find this short analysis stimulates thought and self-observation, and enables you to extend and sharpen your classroom management techniques.

The individual and the craft

Like every other teacher, you and I are individuals with personalities of our own and some teaching approaches which are special to us. Certainly no one can take over another teacher's ways lock, stock, and barrel, apply them, and hope for success. No doubt you will do some extraordinary things that others would not dare to do, and no doubt you will get away with some of them. *But* there are many techniques of class management for the secondary school that can be distilled from the work of hundreds of teachers and observational analysis that have almost universal validity. These are not techniques that will cramp personal style, but ones that will allow it to flower. The paradox is that good *classroom* management makes *personal* teaching possible, for it frees the individual from constant conflict, and only then can the teacher be truly personal. Good organization in the classroom not only avoids confrontation, but it allows the teacher to establish the warm, collaborative relationships with most of the pupils that will facilitate true communication.

The central point is one that does not always sound appealing to a new teacher fired by enthusiasm for a subject and keen to enthuse students. It is embodied in the perhaps uncomfortable word 'management': *the highest aspirations of teaching rest on good classroom management.* Everything depends on good order. Without it every lesson will be an exhausting battle. You will be exhausted; your pupils will behave badly, and later criticize *you* for their bad behaviour. If you establish good order, you can be more subtle, more friendly, and more yourself. Without it a teacher can not meet that very first, over-arching 'Professional Standard' set out for those reaching QTS:

> 'They have high expectations of all pupils; respect their
> social, cultural, linguistic, religious and ethnic backgrounds;
> and are committed to raising their educational
> achievement.'[1]

You regularly find in schools pupils who defy and taunt any teachers who are apparently unable to manage them, and then complain bitterly to parents and senior teachers that they do not like those teachers' classes: 'He doesn't keep us in order!' There is no doubt that a certain proportion of adolescent pupils will try to drive a teacher to distraction; if they succeed they will despise him or her and hate the conditions they have helped to create. Contrary to the impressions some like to give, most, very nearly all, pupils like good order, and are happier if the classroom is 'in control'.

Freedom and control

The very word 'control' is unfashionable and has pejorative associations. Yet as a teacher you must face up to the fact that 'controlling' is part of your task, and if you fail in that you will fail in much else. There is no way in which you can avoid influencing children, and control is certainly not abused just because it is practised. If a teacher's psychological make-up is such that he finds the notion repugnant, he should reconsider his profession. On the other hand, inappropriate 'control' can be counter-productive and a class 'controlled' into inactivity is not one that can learn.

Conversely, a few teachers learn to live with noise, and forget that the teacher who can manage to put up with interruptive noise is often imposing unpleasant and unacceptable conditions upon pupils who cannot. One of the most important freedoms which a school can offer to pupils is freedom from the noise of others, the interruptions of others, and their own restlessness. Of course, good order is certainly not an end in itself, but do not in any way underestimate its value as an aid to your more important aims. Furthermore, good order can be used to create active classes in which group discussion, role play, experiments, and movement for a purpose are part of the 'good order' and facilitate learning.

Three elements of success

Despite the question often asked about a young teacher, 'How's his discipline?', there is no single, readily identifiable characteristic: 'discipline'. The pupils know which teachers 'keep us in order', and those teachers are the ones they are most likely to respect. The pupils cannot usually identify what it is about a particular teacher that leads to this quality of keeping order they admire. Pushed, pupils will offer such helpful clues as: 'Well, she means what she says', 'He knows what he's doing', 'She don't let us muck about', 'We have to get on with things with her'. The insistent questioner will probably put the major part of the elusive quality down to 'personality'. But a careful questioner will also detect at least three other strands amongst the pupils' descriptions of the teachers whom they judge to be a success:

1   The successful teacher cares

One will be a sense of caring, of never giving up. The successful teacher knows that some of his hopes are rarely attainable, but he is not daunted. The pupils sense that this teacher cares and that he will keep on trying, and that he respects them. Such a teacher shows neither signs of exasperation nor resignation. This sense of caring is also conveyed clearly to the pupils in the other sense of whether the teacher 'cares for' them. Many teachers with high ideals fail to feel or demonstrate sufficient care for their charges. Many experienced teachers even use the word 'love' and feel a real sense of love for most of their pupils. Love alone cannot guarantee success, but it is necessary – a rather hard, remote, balanced, ungushing kind of love.

2   The successful teacher teaches well

The second strand the questioner will pick up from the pupils' remarks is that simple one of good basic teaching: 'She makes things clear.' Some people try hard to get close to the pupils, sympathize with their problems, and chat with them, but they fail in their fundamental task of making complicated things simple, of explaining in ways that can be understood, of *teaching*. With some people the word 'didactic' has also become pejorative, and a certain number of teachers mis-apply the value of 'bringing out' the pupil's thinking, and enabling a pupil to see for herself, to a point where they simply do not explain properly. The really knowledgeable person can usually put a complex and deep matter in a few straightforward words.

Although this book is not about curriculum content, it is important to stress that a school 'subject' (better named a 'course') is not intended by the concept of the National Curriculum or any statutory orders to have to be co-terminous with the content of the definition of the National Curriculum 'subject'. Indeed, the QCA's texts make it clear that key skills, such as literacy, numeracy, and ICT, should be woven into all courses.[4] Similarly, social, artistic, and ethical points can properly be related to many aspects of your subject teaching. Indeed, Citizenship should be a part of all courses. In putting across your 'subject' you can benefit from bringing in wider aspects of human interest and knowledge – as well as your own enthusiasms.

3 The successful teacher manages well

The third strand, however, is the one with which this book is most fully concerned: a good teacher is a good classroom manager. Whatever mode of teaching she or he is employing, and whatever subject matter or skill is being explored, a teacher's first task is managing the classroom. This includes the planning of the environment, the planning of the time, the relating of the curriculum content to specific learning activities, the organization of study materials, and the control of the group. It also involves the teacher's own voice and manner.

This book argues that these features combine to create 'the craft of the classroom', and that this craft is a necessary one for the teacher, and one about which much can be taught and learnt. The craft of the classroom is something at which you can work and at which you can get better. In doing so you will not only increase your control of the classroom, but paradoxically, you will also find yourself giving less attention to class management, getting closer to the pupils, teaching more helpfully, and enjoying the pupils more. Good relationships are to some extent an ingredient of successful classroom management, but to a considerable degree they are also the *result*. There is more crossness, shouting, and criticism in a badly run classroom than a good one. The well-organized teacher is in a better position to be pleasant to the pupils. A mastery of group management techniques frees a teacher from concerns about group control and facilitates collaboration. Furthermore, it enables him or her to be more creative, stimulate better concentration, develop stronger learning, and increase the pupils' actual enjoyment of the learning.

Being prepared

Some of the techniques I outline in this book are easier to describe than to do. Practice will make them possible but you will find the task easier for pre-planning. One of the paradoxes of classroom management is that some initial fuss often reduces subsequent fuss; that some apparently complicated initial procedures actually simplify procedures in the long run; that formal routines free the sessions for close relationships. To be organized and firm is to have cleared the decks for variety of activity and friendliness, but to be slightly confused and wavering is to produce a muddle that will lead only to frayed tempers, cross words, less pupil enjoyment, and less learning.

All this is especially true with less well-motivated and with 'difficult' children. For them your technique must be impeccable. I have seen teachers trying to muddle through for years: it doesn't work. If, on the other hand, you analyse an aspect of classroom management to establish what makes it difficult, you will usually see where the difficulty lies, and be able to go a long way towards avoiding it next time round. For instance, contrary to many of our easily adopted attitudes, it isn't the presence of two or three troublesome pupils that makes it difficult to get a lesson started. It is an inherently difficult task whatever the composition of the pupil group, and some teachers would run into difficulties with a hand-picked class of obliging pupils. With any pupils, your class management skill must be as polished as possible. Have no doubt, though, that this is a skill that can be analysed, the component parts practised, and the overall skill learnt. (This can be done partly on your own, but more helpfully with a colleague, whether as your Induction Tutor or as part of the wider Performance Management process.)

There is, then, a craft of classroom management, which is independent not only of subject, but also of mode of teaching, and applies to your handling of your Tutor Group as much as a course subject. Whatever you are teaching, *and however you plan to teach*, you must run a good classroom.

2

The relationships of the classroom

Of all the sections of this book, clearly the one in which I attempt to discuss how to create 'good relationships' with pupils is the most difficult. Here is the nub of the teacher's task, yet it is the most difficult to define, the most personal to achieve, and the most intangible to judge. Advice can easily be misapplied, and remarks parodied. Yet I must attempt the task, both because it is so important and because I believe that the creation of good classroom relationships is actually more amenable to technical advice than it may seem to be. It is not luck but method which brings success. Good relationships are in fact *created* largely by technique, although that is strongly enriched by the teacher's personal attitude.

Very reasonably, the Professional Standards for QTS specify key aspects of relationships with pupils, requiring of those awarded QTS that:

> 'They treat pupils consistently, with respect and consideration, and are concerned with their development as learners.'[1]

In the 'Teaching and Class Management' section the overall requirement is clearly set out, requiring of teachers that:

> 'They set high expectations for pupils' behaviour and establish a clear framework for classroom discipline to anticipate and manage pupils' behaviour constructively, and promote self-control and independence.'[1]

There is also a sound emphasis on the connection between the teacher as a *model* of good inter-personal relationships and specifically teaching behaviour, requiring of teachers that:

> 'They demonstrate and promote the positive values,
> attitudes and behaviour that they expect from their pupils.'[1]

These requirements are very important, and working to achieve them is personally rewarding, though considerable self-reflection and analysis is required. The supporting *Handbook of Guidance* backs this crucial requirement up by examples of the values which can be expected:

> 'Respect for other people; a positive attitude towards
> learning; respect for cultural diversity; care for the
> environment; and social responsibility.'

It also illustrates some of the ways in which these values will be demonstrated:

> 'Trainee teachers are expected to understand the values and
> attitudes that they want pupils to develop, reflecting the
> culture and ethos of the school in which they work. Trainee
> teachers should put these values into practice, both in the
> classroom and in the wider school context.'[6]

The early TTA draft gave further advice on how to have concern for the pupils' 'development as learners', which is to:

> 'identify and build on pupils' personal qualities, particular
> interests and learning styles;'
> 'enable pupils to understand the relevance of their learning
> in school to life beyond and outside school.'[7]

Both of these aims are at the core of building your classroom relationships.

In the first place, though, do not presume that it is as easy as all that; do not presume that you are the first pleasant person who has come the way of these pupils; and, above all, do not presume that your *will* to create good relationships will prove sufficient. You will need to work at it patiently and skilfully; you will need to have a long-term perspective; and you will need to have created an orderly and systematic classroom procedure which allows the good relationship.

Remember who you are

Focus quite clearly on the obvious but easily overlooked fact that it is as a *teacher* that you are hoping to create a relationship. The teaching is not only the object of the exercise, it is also the special gift that *you* have for the pupil and which most of the other people to whom the pupil relates have not got. This is both a proud claim and a modest one.

It is arrogant to forget that, although on occasions you will do some mothering, most of your pupils have splendid mothers; although on occasions you will be matey, most of your pupils have close friends with whom they spend hours; although on occasions you will be avuncular, most of your pupils have adequate uncle figures.

Do not let your knowledge of the very sad cases of some children from broken, confused, or uncaring homes tempt you into forgetting that the majority of pupils have warm and supportive homes. Do not allow your wish to be a friend to come between you as teacher and pupil: if you cannot succeed as a teacher, your friendship is unlikely to be of special value to the young person.

A teacher opens up unknown or only half-suspected areas of skill or knowledge: you make things clear; you make things as simple as possible. Above all, you enable pupils to do more things and to do them better, to understand more things and to understand them better. Only if you are felt to be successful in these teacherly ways will the pupils warm to you.

It is therefore doubly misjudged to allow the wish for 'a good relationship' to hinder effective teaching. There is an understandable but unhelpful tendency towards circular explanations: 'Jason talks a lot because he's an extrovert', 'Millie is a pest because she gets no support at home' ... and so on. These attempts at social or psychological explanation, even if they have some intellectual attraction, can short-circuit the planning of effective classroom management strategies.

Relating to classroom behaviour

Whilst it is an appropriate professional approach to speculate on causes that may lie behind a pupil's classroom behaviour, two points need stressing: firstly, that speculation is not amenable to proof – the mixture of reasons is likely to be multi-factorial and could be significantly different from that hypothesized. Secondly, whatever external, contributory influences, our professional responsibility is for the classroom context. The same pupil can be observed behaving very differently in the classrooms of different teachers. Our concern is to create the most positive environment. The teacher has considerable control over the whole life of the classroom – only very extreme pupils are not largely influenced by it. To over-emphasize external causes can lead to avoiding the specific teaching necessitated by the behaviour presented.

In this respect it is also important to avoid a well-meant but essentially patronizing social 'determinism' that allows teachers to collude with pupils from less well-off backgrounds to avoid real learning as 'irrelevant' or beyond them.

In the last few decades teachers have become far more socially aware. There are few of us who have not read the important analyses of the educational psychologists and sociologists. This is a distinct gain. However, for some teachers it can get between them and their task. It is easy to misuse sociological information, especially analyses of the characteristics of social class. We now know something of the educational handicaps of some children of unskilled and semi-skilled workers, children of minority ethnic background, one-parent families, and other deprived groups.

Less well known, but very important for developing relationships with some pupils, is the deep and continuing effect on a youngster's attitude and behaviour if, as a *one*-year-old, he or she suffered from lack of 'security of attachment'. The prime care-giver (usually the mother) who does not relate closely, warmly and empathetically to the baby often creates a lasting gap in the growing child's inter-personal understanding and skills. (The full explanation of a baby's need for 'security of attachment' is well explained by the originator of the concept, which is now used widely in clinical work and in supporting refugee children, John Bowlby.[8])

A single teacher cannot compensate fully of course for any problems created by the youngster having missed out on security of attachment as a young child. However, each teacher's involved, empathetic, and committed relationship truly and sometimes deeply helps. You, of course, remain 'a teacher' and do not become a member of the family. Nevertheless, there are times when a youngster will share worries with you precisely because you have that distance of the teacherly role. Strong empathy is not incompatible with a certain distance and the retention of the professional position.

This knowledge of the range of upbringing difficulties is very occasionally misused to create an oversimplified kind of 'determinism', which is allowed to trap pupils in their current plight: 'You can't expect high literacy standards. Look at their homes,' or 'There's nothing relevant in the curriculum for them, so naturally they aren't motivated to do homework.' Such attitudes are helpful only if they are used to sharpen our techniques and create sympathy. They are dangerous if they lead us to treat pupils as if school had nothing but sympathy to offer. What I have come to call 'inverse snobbism' and 'inverse racism' can undermine a teacher's approach to pupils. For these pupils as much as any others, the teacher must teach and must maintain with cheerful determination the aim of making learning possible.

Considering motivation

You will want to consider continuously the motivation of the classroom. We have rightly elevated motivation to a high priority in our planning. It is important, however, that in searching for improved motivation we do not overlook the very basic point that almost the best motivation is simply achievement. On the whole, we want to do the things we can do, and do not want to do the things we cannot do. In classroom terms this means that it is not practical to put too much emphasis on motivation, nor to wait until pupils 'are motivated' to do something. Vigorous teaching of the skills will often lead on to motivation. 'Being able' to do is very close to 'wanting' to do. Not being able to do is distressingly off-putting.

The child-centred 'interest' model gave a great deal of good to education, but it is not only inadequate in itself, but can be positively harmful if not carefully used. We must not assume that the best form of motivation is to re-shape the curriculum so that the learning can be more 'relevant'.

As adults we have four main reward systems: money, usefulness, status, and the gratitude or approval of those we live with. The teenager, poised apparently functionless in the world, has few possible rewards in school. Money is only a useful motivation for some aspects of some subjects (and there is a limit to the possible extension of this reward system); status is in a way available; it is, however, the gratitude or approval of those we live with that is the most potent: the second greatest motivation (that is, after achievement) is the pupil's relationship with his teachers. School is part of life (not mere preparation for it) and works only if it offers human warmth and satisfaction. The teacher's task is to recognize this and build it into her systems. By using this, she can both make the learning more effective *and* create a satisfying social life. Thus, teaching style and effective class management actually increase the pupils' motivation.

Some attitude problems

There is amongst some young teachers a diffidence that makes them pull back from imposing their will: the result, too often, is that a clique of pupils in the class imposes its will instead. This is resented by the other pupils, and the resentment sours those pupils' relationship with the teacher. Diffidence is a virtue in many circumstances, but it is dangerous in the classroom: it often allows those who are not diffident – and there are likely to be a few in every group – to dominate. This leads to tension, conflict, rows, and in the end to a less pleasant and tighter domination by the teacher if she can achieve it. If not, the situation is left unresolved in an excess of bad temper. Conversely, some teachers are over-insistent about imposing their will, and reprimand insistently and sharply over the trivial. One observer of a lesson commented that the teacher kept demanding 'Less noise!' when hardly any was being made.

There is also a very understandable fear which many teachers have of losing the affection of or good relationship with pupils. This fear makes the teachers, like timid lovers, apprehensive lest the first dark look is evidence of favours withdrawn forever. A stress on creating good relationships with those being taught can be self-defeating if it leads the teacher to go for quick results, and encourages him to reduce his demands in the hope of easier returns. It is sad to see a desperately anxious teacher casting away more and more of his standards and sacrificing the elements essential to a good long-term relationship to the empty hopes of immediate success.

Teaching is a reasonably long-term activity, and the relationships that succeed will be built up by a consistent policy. The pupil is always suggesting that he will withdraw his affection from the teacher, like the child from his parent, unless a demand is dropped. If your demand is legitimate and for the pupil's good, don't be tempted to abandon it. The relationships at which you should be aiming are those achieved by, say, the end of the term, not the end of the first week.

Getting to know your pupils

The first task is to learn their names. It really helps if you know each of your pupils by his or her correct, used name as early as possible – and that means getting the abbreviations right too. The school needs the full, correct name for its record, for instance for examination entries. You should, however, normally use the 'known as' name, which most (but sadly not all) schools establish and note at the initial interview. It is sometimes difficult to remember that a boy or girl does not always have the same last name as their parents or carers. For instance, some couples maintain the use of their own family names and the woman does not take the married surname. Mothers and fathers have different last names in Islamic families. And so on. What is more, some 'known as' abbreviations are a little difficult to remember, and for the Anglophone teacher Asian names can be difficult to pronounce. I recommend practising saying the names aloud to yourself. If you find that you are still hesitating or stumbling over pronunciation, ask the pupil to help you. Do not push your difficulty to one side.

A few initial mistakes do not actually matter. They are inevitable, and accepted by the pupils as evidence that you are trying. Laugh at your mistakes, and come back to another attempt fairly soon.

For years I used to write my memory off blandly as 'never good with pupils' names', as if it was a regrettable but inevitable, inherent failing. The result was that I had unnecessary difficulties with classes for far too long. I now realize that there are positive steps you can take to help yourself.

- Study the list of pupils in advance, and when you are copying it into your mark-book, or on to seating plans, and so on, try to memorize the name-surname combinations.
- Pay particular attention to naming systems from linguistic backgrounds with which you are not familiar.
- It helps to know as many first names as possible, even before you have met the pupils. When you study the records and files, use this also as a conscious name-learning session.
- In the classroom (and your seating plan helps here) do not use the fact you have not yet learnt the names by pointing at pupils to whom you want to speak. Use names from the very first by glancing down at your seating plan.
- Some teachers ask pupils to have their exercise books or folders displayed on their desks so that they can glance at their names. Others ask new classes to make name cards for their desks. These can also help.
- Give back exercise books yourself as part of your memorization.

Some teachers involve pupils in name learning games, for example, stopping lessons five minutes early and not dismissing the class until the teacher has remembered all the names. This gives the whole class a vested interest in the success of the teacher and shows that the teacher values the exercise.

You will rarely or never get to know pupils as people via the whole group or with the whole group present. Obviously, your observation of each of them in the group context will contribute massively to your knowledge of each individual pupil. Just as obviously, you will learn a great deal from reading the assignments which are done for you. Clearly, you will need to supplement this direct observation by studying the background of each pupil. This can be time consuming if done thoroughly, but as each year you stay at the school you carry forward your knowledge of many of the pupils, the problem decreases.

The two obvious ways of filling in on the background of your pupils are by consulting the files or record cards (either those held by your department or those held by the pastoral organization) and by discussing the list of pupils with the pastoral figure (in almost all schools that is the 'Tutor') of each class. This does, of course, take a lot of time. If you specifically ask for background details, and not classroom behaviour, you will glean much helpful information. If you have six classes, as you may, I advise you to enquire methodically about each group in turn at the rate of about two a week, and be satisfied with a fairly short session to get the basic material you need. Jot down each point, however briefly, for you will never remember all that you pick up.

Pupils assessed by the school's specialists as having SEN require additional study. You will need to make 'Individual Education Plans' for those in your classes. It is often helpful to study those pupils' full files and to consider the IEPs devised by other subject teachers for them.

Some schools have specially convened meetings of all the teachers concerned with a particular group of pupils. These are sometimes chaired by the Tutor, sometimes by a Head of Year, Head of House, or more senior member of staff. Obviously such meetings are of immense value in sharing knowledge of each pupil. Take these opportunities, and as often as possible talk to your colleagues about the pupils and try to see some of their work in other courses.

Despite the importance of methodically using these ways of getting to know your pupils, there is obviously nothing as valuable as personal knowledge. This comes from your using every possible opportunity to talk one-to-one, or, at the most, with two pupils at a time. There will be some chances within the lesson as you circulate or call pupils to sit by you. But these moments must be built upon by creating as many additional out-of-class opportunities as possible. Start this as soon as you can by asking one or two members of the group to stay behind afterwards, perhaps to help you with some task, perhaps just to talk over their work. Do not make a dead set at the very start at the handful of obviously difficult pupils, but on the other hand do try to get these pupils for a chat fairly early on. And then, do not overdo it: you are not going to find out all their secrets and establish a warm, lasting relationship in five minutes of arranging a wall display or chatting over a piece of homework. You have succeeded well enough if you get to know your chosen pupil just a little more than you did. Then you have begun to break down that frightening 'class' into individuals.

By patiently working at each and every opportunity, you will gradually build up a close knowledge of each pupil, and will find that when you are working with the whole class, in addition to the class management lines, you have also, as it were, a series of private lines, a rich network of personal relationships of different degrees of strength. Everything you do to extend and deepen this network further should be of great help and satisfaction to you.

Using your 'duty' times

One unexpected source of knowledge will come your way, if you make the effort, through your responsibilities under whatever 'duty' rota system your school runs. It is too easy, but quite wrong, to think of a teacher's supervisory 'duties' as mere chores that in some utopia will be handed over to other figures. Playground, corridor, or lunch-hall duties are essentially *teaching* activities. They are opportunities for relating to pupils in a variety of contexts. A duty is wasted if you just stand and look on coolly. You can find out about individual pupils by stopping to exchange a word, or by having an extended conversation. You will find out how to speak to pupils in joke or in anger, and how to influence them with good grace. Although supervisory duties can be difficult, you will learn a great deal without the constraints of the classroom, without problems of class management, and without the demands of the curriculum.

Supervisory duties are often a strain to young teachers, who find it difficult to establish their role and are frankly nervous about precisely how observant they should be, how strict they should be, and what manner they should adopt. In the first place, it is important to remember that the bunch of unknown boys whom you see lurking in that funny corner behind the gyms might well be your responsibility in a classroom soon, either in a regular class of yours or in a lesson you are having to cover for an absent teacher. When you do meet them, they will remember their playground encounter. If you avoid them, obviously unsure of your ground, they will take their future cue from your present behaviour. You must weigh in to any trouble or incipient trouble that you see, however slight or however serious.

Carefully check in advance precisely what is allowed and what is not (for example: Is the grass protected? Can ball games be played anywhere?). Move definitely but calmly towards any group of pupils, especially if they are in odd corners or recesses. Go in smiling, if possible making a joke or a cheerful conversational remark. Unless there is clearly harm being done, do not necessarily investigate. Keep the conversation going and disperse the group good-humouredly.

A large amount of a school's bullying takes place during these sessions, especially in the less well supervised corners of staircases and school grounds. Watch very carefully and do not accept any oral or physical aggression to other pupils. If you do see any misbehaviour (for example, fighting or damage to the building), act firmly. If you are very new and do not know the pupils, send another pupil for the senior teacher likely to be available. If you feel you can cope, tell the pupils suspected of the bad behaviour to come with you to the senior teacher.

Support staff

Staff working in a school and with a school include many who are not formally 'teachers', yet whose work is very important indeed both to teachers and for their contribution to the all-round learning of the pupils. Public discussion typically plays down the significance of the full range of staff in a school. Sadly, the old tradition amongst many teachers was to undervalue their contribution and some teachers belittled the 'non-teaching staff'. In the twenty-first century there has valuably been a substantial expansion of teaching assistants in the classroom, especially for EAL pupils and those with SEN. There has also been an expansion of specialists working for the LEA or a range of agencies.

Your relationship with pupils and their families and your work with your pupils is immensely strengthened if you work well with the school support staff and the visiting professionals. Indeed, the style of your relationship with them does not only help your working with them, but also is a model for the pupils. A pupil will notice how a teacher talks to the Receptionist or the Premises Manager – and will learn from it. There have been what I call 'professio-centric' teachers, who demonstrate to the pupils poor interpersonal relationships when they are talking with support staff.

Since 2002 the ability to work with this range of people has been formally incorporated into the standards required for QTS; one of which under 'Professional Values and Practice' is:

> 'They understand the contribution that support staff and other professionals make to teaching and learning.'[1]

This is further explored in the *Handbook of Guidance*. It thoughtfully expands the brief summary statement quoted above, giving a page of requirements. The first of the following paragraphs included sets out the professional standards expected and the second the kinds of evidence that should be used to assess the NQT during her or his induction year:

> 'The care and education of pupils are often the collective responsibility of a network of professionals and other support staff. Teachers need, therefore, to have some understanding of how other adults, both within the classroom and beyond, can contribute to teaching and learning, and how teachers can use this contribution as a resource. This understanding assumes awareness of other colleagues' roles, and how a teacher's responsibilities relate to and complement those of others. This will include an ability to recognise the limits of their own expertise and authority and an awareness of when and how to seek help from a colleague.'
>
> Can the trainee teacher establish collaborative working relationships? Does the trainee have a clear idea of how the teacher's role relates to that of other team members? These sources can also indicate the trainee teacher's understanding of the distinct roles and responsibilities of other professionals including, for example, social workers, educational

psychologists, educational welfare officers, youth justice workers, school nurses or other health professionals.'[6]

From my own experience and observation of successful and unsuccessful collaboration, and in the light of my judgement that the whole range of support staff are very important to the education of the pupils, I should stress the following key points:

i   ensure you know the full range of her or his responsibilities;
ii keep her or him fully informed about the matter on which you are seeking help, and do not merely use him or her as a minor underling;
iii arrange for appropriate praise and appreciation to be given – by yourself and on occasions by seniors;
iv show respect and appropriate warmth to all those with whom you are collaborating.

With classroom assistants and with technicians (in Science, PE, D&T, and sometimes the arts courses) 'classroom management' includes the need to 'manage the work of teaching assistants or other adults to enhance pupils' learning'[7]. This is a difficult skill and one which it can be difficult to learn and have experience of in training. The 'management' needs to include the following:

i   ensure that you fully brief the assistants on the aim of the lesson sequence, how it relates to the overall aims of the course, and the special emphases you intend;
ii when possible, incorporate the assistants in the planning of sequences of lessons;
iii agree the precise roles of the assistants, according to the function, for example, general teaching assistants, EAL specialist, SEN support for an individual pupil or pupils, technicians;
iv introduce them fully to the class;
v   draw on their own specialism and knowledge for the whole class's benefit when appropriate;
vi plan how they will time and fit their individual work with a pupil to the whole-class presentation you are making.

Working with various support staff who have knowledge, experience, or skills that you have not had the opportunity to gain is one of the satisfactions of teaching in many schools, and can be a real pleasure if you are appreciative and have the keenness to participate in and use those attributes. You will work from time to time (especially in your tutorial role), for instance, with specialist agency staff from a family therapy centre or a unit for pupils with extreme social difficulties, and also with EAL and SEN specialists. A strong teacher recognizes their capacities and enjoys working with them. Somewhat similarly, technicians, for instance in D&T, Science, and the Performing Arts, will have some skills and knowledge that even an experienced specialist teacher does not have. Some teachers are perhaps less ready to recognize that there will also be times when classroom assistants may have insights, experiences, and capacities that they do not themselves have. These may have derived from their training and experience in other occupations, but they may also have come from human experiences that simply have not come your way in life, such as being bilingual, immigrating from another country, having a strong enthusiasm for a particular hobby, having had an unusual childhood upbringing, having children of their own, and so on. Recognizing the special strengths of others does not in any way undermine you as a teacher. Not recognizing special attributes and the contribution that these people can thus make to your work and to the development of your pupils may both reduce your deeper authority and weaken the strength of your contribution to the education of your pupils.

Your work for the pupils whom you teach your subject and for whom you are their tutor, and your handling of classroom management will be deeply strengthened if you understand and respect their contribution, brief them carefully, and incorporate their contribution fully.

Beyond-timetable activities

There is one whole range of activities which deserves special mention as a way of getting to know pupils – the many things that often live under the vague title 'extra-curricular activities'. (This is still the most common term, though it is misleading as they are part of the school curriculum in its full sense.) A number of schools and other organizations prefer to use the terms 'Beyond-timetable' or 'Extra time'.

It is probably wise in your first year not to devote too much precious energy to beyond-timetable activities, and certainly not to over-burden yourself with the taxing worry of actually organizing or leading such an activity. Nevertheless, I would stress that it is in the shared enthusiasms of camping, sports, producing plays, tidying books, playing chess, playing music, looking after animals, kicking a ball around, or going to the theatre that teacher and taught can come closest together. This is part of the justification for the inclusion in the specification of the 'Professional Standards for QTS' that:

> 'They can contribute to, and share responsibility in, the corporate life of schools.'[1]

The corporate life of the school feeds into the success of the classroom and is an extension of it – truly part of the delivery of the whole-school curriculum.

This will be a valuable investment for you in two ways. On the one hand, you will have a sprinkling of allies in various parts of the school with whom you have forged bonds in their special cherished circumstances. And on the other hand, you will have learned a great deal about young people, their reactions, and their moods. You will have learnt how to speak to pupils in a variety of contexts, when to quip and when to be serious, when to turn a blind eye and when to be eagle-eyed, when to muck in and when to rise above. Above all, you will have learnt how to lay down limits and say 'No' when necessary in ways which are acceptable. You will, it is true, have learnt all this with a rather special selection of pupils, but what you will have learnt can be applied to your relations with all of them. I should go as far as to say that you are less likely to succeed in the classroom if you have not gained that special dimension from some beyond-timetable activities.

Consistency

It is harder in fact than in theory to establish a reasonably consistent regime, but it is essential to do so if you are to create good relationships. Pupils like to know where they are with their teachers, and not be pulled up one day for what they were allowed to get away with the day before. Agreement between teachers is difficult to achieve and less essential. Obviously a wildly different set of expectations between teachers is not desirable, but just as pupils accept differences between behaviour codes in laboratories and libraries, so they expect and can accept a certain degree of difference between teachers. The staff of school should work towards reducing these differences by discussion and debate, but obviously they will never be removed completely. This the pupils will accept. But they do *not* find differences within a single teacher's behaviour acceptable. 'Moody' is a serious criticism, and justifiably so. To be allowed to talk after a 'Silence' one day, but to be reprimanded for the same talking in the same situation the following day causes both confusion and resentment. Try hard to set unvarying standards: always get cross with late-comers; always make a fuss about homework not brought; never accept talking during a declared 'silent' session; and so on. If your rules are reasonable, stick to them day in and day out.

When all is said and done, however, you will have to vary your approach to suit the individuals you teach. You must be consistent from occasion to occasion, but flexible from individual to individual. One of the specialisms of a school is that of knowing pupils. You will subtly vary your approach to each as you get to know him or her. With one you will need to remain always light-hearted, with another quiet and personal. One may require only a look, another a sharp remark. You will learn that some pupils react badly to public rebuke, some cannot stand praise in public, others will not answer questions aloud however hard you press, whilst some will try to answer a question before you have even asked it. Many pupils behave acceptably but cannot resist subtly baiting to provoke. The teacher who knows those pupils intimately knows how to sidestep the provocation, retain dignity and authority, and maintain a warm relationship. All this requires empathy and a great flexibility of approach to individuals.

Be determined. A teacher must never give up. If your pupils know that you know clearly and without doubt who has not done something, their confidence in your knowledge is the first, and remarkably successful, 'disciplinary' influence you have. The second is their certainty that you will not give up. Most pupils are canny enough to know that with many teachers a 'forgotten' piece of homework not brought one day will mean the end of the matter. If it is clear that the teacher will remember and ask for it the following day – and keep on until it has been obtained – the number of initial lapses of memory drops impressively. Significantly, skipping lessons during the day ('post-registration truancy') has been shown by national research to vary from teacher to teacher according to the pupils' perception of the teachers; spotting and checking of lesson absence.[9] In general, never let anything go by you and there will be less to chase. The more fuss you make, the less you will have to fuss about.

Praise and ...

Undoubtedly, we are all happier and do better when we are praised rather than criticized. Much of what I have said in previous sections has been designed to put pupils in situations in which they can legitimately be praised and to keep them out of situations in which they are likely to behave badly and thus bring criticism on themselves from even the mildest or more forbearing of teachers. If this has been achieved, make sure that the ratio of praise to censure remains squarely in favour of praise. Both individuals and the class as a whole need to be commended for their achievements.

We teachers are strangely selective in what we praise and whom we praise. One study showed that 20% of the teachers observed gave no approval for social behaviour at all! Of teacher responses, the overall rate of approval to disapproval was 60% 'academic' related, with a ratio of 45 to 15 approval to disapproval, whereas of the 40% of responses that were 'classroom behaviour' related, the ratio dramatically reversed, with 30% of the *overall* responses being of disapproval. Only 10% of all the teacher responses praised behaviour. As the observer remarked: 'Pupils are clearly expected to behave well and are continually reprimanded if they do not.'[10]

It is easy to overlook the occasions for praise, and to react more rapidly to the need to censure. Remember to praise the ordinary.

Personal praise is certainly possible: a pupil dressed particularly smartly, a polite or helpful gesture or action, a new hairstyle, a new school bag, a well-labelled exercise book. Each lesson, you should try to find some word of praise for a handful of fairly ordinary but commendable things: a well-answered question, the good use of a word, a helpful act, kindness to another pupil. However, praise is not a mere tool to be used for management. Indeed, there is evidence that blanket, undifferentiated, and too easily won praise can be counter-productive. Closely-focused and very specific individual praise is the most effective.

There are three audience contexts for praise, and they should all be used for really good effect. Firstly, there is the public praise in front of the other pupils. This is sometimes appreciated, but should not be overdone or loosely fulsome. Indeed, its likely effect on the inter-relationships of the community of the class always needs consideration. Secondly, there is the quiet private word with the individual pupil. This is too often forgotten. Sometimes it should be used to reinforce the first, perhaps on the way out at the end of the lesson. Thirdly, there is the communication of praise by note or entry in the school Diary for parent or Tutor (Form Teacher) to see. Again, do not forget this very helpful act. Parents very much like to and need to hear good reports of their children.

Be careful how you praise the regular public troublemaker. If, as is so often the case, he or she is seeking group status by ostentatious misbehaviour, the pupil will resent the public praise as an attack on the hard-earned bad reputation, and as likely as not will find some technique of expression or gesture that not only nullifies the praise but, worse than that, actually associates your praise with his or her scorn – thus devaluing it for others. Pupils can publicly 'do dirt' on your commendation, and this is potentially dangerous for the future. This does not, however, normally mean that they do not want the praise, merely that they do not want it openly. For such a pupil the private word of praise is better, and frequently effective.

... criticism

Generally speaking, when you need to criticize do it clearly but briefly, do not dwell on it, and, above all, avoid a tirade of abuse directed publicly at an individual. Such a tirade creates a deep resentment in the individual so that, far from being persuaded to mend his ways, he will harden against you and feel justified in his action. Added to that, other individuals will sympathize with the victim in his plight, and you will have lost the goodwill of a whole section of the class. Whenever you respond publicly to a pupil, you must also have in mind the ripple effect on the other pupils.

Do not focus over-sharply on the regular troublemakers. The American theorist Harvey Clarizio[11] dubs one technique 'extinction'. He means by this the ignoring of the troublesome behaviour to avoid rewarding it by taking notice. This is a line which should be used only with care – but it reminds one that it is possible actually to reinforce bad behaviour by giving it inappropriate attention.

Whenever possible, influence the misbehaving pupil, or the pupil about to misbehave, silently and without the rest of the class knowing. Perhaps a small gesture will catch his eye; more likely a stare will be sensed and he will look up. Then a mere continuation of the stare may be sufficient, but it can be strengthened by a frown, or even a smile. This last may sound surprising, but a smile indicates you know the pupil was up to something she should not have been, that you are not furious – yet, and that if she stops all will be well. A mouthed but soundless word or two can also be added occasionally. Such tactics avoid advertising the unsuitable behaviour to other pupils, and avoid the attendant risk of encouraging others to join in. They also avoid you adding your voice to the disturbance. This even creates a conspiratorial feeling between you and the would-be wrongdoer that leaves a pleasurable rather than a thwarted feeling in the pupil. One warning, though: if you use the stare as a device, do not be outstared back – you must win.

Observational studies of discipline in schools have shown that girls are typically reprimanded at a lower threshold of poor behaviour than boys – usually because better behaviour is expected of them. It used to be argued that this was unfair on girls, and in some ways it is, for instance if the reprimand is unpleasantly put across. However, I have come to consider that the opposite is true: from the earliest years there is a tendency for parents and carers to expect somewhat better behaviour, less noise, and more understanding personal responses from girls. (This is especially true when there are two, three, or more sons and daughters of somewhat similar ages: an oldest boy or a boy who is the only child is often treated by parents and carers more like girls are treated.) In classrooms from the early primary years there is similarly a difference in expectation of behaviour between boys and girls – perhaps until the sixth form. This has a bad effect on boys and their continuing bad behaviour, which tends to lead to lower attainment and create a far greater risk of punishment. This can be seen as growing from this near encouragement of expected poor behaviour by waiting until their behaviour reaches a higher level before reprimanding. It is the boys in those classrooms who are being treated 'unfairly', not the girls! Somewhat similarly, in multi-ethnic schools some studies have shown that there can be a tendency to see the misdemeanours of children of minority ethnic background more rapidly and more often than their white peers. This has been argued as one of the reasons why, for instance, children of African-Caribbean background are more likely to be punished, and even excluded, than their white peers. My observation and experience has led me to judge the opposite: many well-intentioned teachers, anxious to be 'inclusive' and 'anti-racist', permit a higher threshold level of misbehaviour before they reprimand. I have come to see this as a form of what I call 'inverse racism' as it actually encourages those African-Caribbean boys to act the part expected of them by many fellow pupils, and also further encourages those other pupils in that expectation of troublesome behaviour. This leads the African-Caribbean boys to reach the punishable threshold more rapidly. The teacher's expectation of behaviour, the observation, and the response must be as consistently fair as possible.

Avoiding confrontation

Many disturbances that are minor but nevertheless require more than a look or silent gesture are quelled easily by the teacher who shows he or she is anxious to get on with the job in hand and is not willing to waste time investigating. A Science teacher moving towards a group whose experiment is being held back by giggles over something one of the boys has produced from his pocket would actually be best advised to say as he arrived at the group: 'Come on; we just haven't got time for that', and immediately ask an interesting question about the experiment. In general, it is more effective to use what has been called 'task-focused' criticisms rather than 'approval-focused', especially as far as the effect on other pupils is concerned:

'Ray, if you talk you won't be able to hear these new words so well' is normally better than:
'Ray, I'm surprised at you letting me down again.'

Criticisms and prohibitions must be specific and clear. It is amazingly easy to convey a general sense of disapproval without making it clear exactly what is being objected to. American research has demonstrated that the clarity of reprimands is of more importance than their intensity. Thus:

'Don't touch that display board' is more likely to be effective than:
'Behave yourself.'

and:

'Leave Gary's desk alone' is more likely to be effective than:
'Stop fooling around.'

Your bluff will usually be called, so do not throw out empty threats of punishments you cannot carry out. Very rarely indeed do teachers use physical threats: 'If you don't sit down, I'll hit you'. It is neither permitted nor desirable to do so. These undermine your authority, create an unpleasant atmosphere and are professionally unacceptable. (I am excepting the occasional *very clearly* jocular threats which really are meant to be, and are, taken as jokes to relieve class tension. Similarly, if you know you have to hurry away after school one day, do not threaten to keep a pupil in unless you are willing to forgo your appointment. Always keep your word to your pupils.

Never allow a situation to go really sour. Whatever may have been done or said, you have to go on working with that pupil for a year or even more. You must therefore firmly resist using words that you cannot recant and which leave you in a posture of irrevocable anger and dislike. You can criticize what he has *done* or *said* or *not done* as strongly as you like (although temperateness is advisable), but you must not venture from his crimes to himself. You must not criticize *him*.

Too often I have come across situations where the teacher has allowed justifiable indignation at an unpleasant action of a pupil to lead to a bitter attack on the overall character of the pupil. I submit that this is unjustified, as the teacher's current task is to define and criticize the action only, and, closer to my present point, it is unwise, as it puts the relationship in a position from which it may never recover. If you put a pupil beyond the pale you are preventing all hope of future communication. Yesterday's action can be forgiven and forgotten, as can yesterday's criticism of it. But yesterday's character assassination has a continuing life, is still significant today, and will be remembered bitterly:

> 'That's a dangerous/time-wasting/silly thing to do' is very much better than:
> 'You're a dangerous/time-wasting/silly person.'

There are some unfair tactics that teachers slip into in the heat of the moment. You may feel that you will never indulge in such unpleasantness, but it is worth being warned so that you can see the temptation coming, and steer away:

- Never refer to a pupil's family in front of other pupils.
- Never use the ill fame of other brothers and sisters, perhaps because they were at the school, to criticize a pupil. Never make invidious comparisons with other members of the family.
- Never refer to physical or 'racial' characteristics.
- Never say anything to wound.

It is sad that some teachers are tempted into offensive, wounding remarks about the pupil as a person. When in a tutorial session, a Year Seven girl misunderstood a public-address announcement about her Year leaving the building; she wrongly stood up when she should have waited for the Tutor's ending of the session and instruction to leave. The Tutor called across the room: 'You're mental!' Such wounding remarks are fairly rare, but you need to practise to yourself suitable terms of criticism and rigorously avoid the personally wounding.

There will sometimes be disobedience from all classes and with all teachers. It is essential to take up the first instance and calmly, fairly, but firmly, prevent it, and punish it. It is far better for all concerned to act on that first instance, however small, rather than to wait until you have to impose unjust, wholesale punishment on the whole of an unruly class. American research into classroom behaviour certainly supports the common sense realization that there are techniques of stopping trouble, and that some teachers are more successful than others, not because of their fierceness or punitiveness, but because of their skill. The researchers in Jacob S. Kounin's study[12] scored hundreds of hours of video-taped lessons according to the ability the teacher had to stop misbehaviour. They invented the term 'withitness', which rather nicely describes the ability of a teacher to communicate to the pupils that he or she knows what is going on. If a teacher can communicate that fact to the class, without necessarily having to declare it aloud, much of the potential trouble will never take place. The teachers who have become immersed in helping an individual, or stopping one bit of trouble, often pick the wrong pupil, especially picking on an appreciative onlooker or an imitative pupil rather than the initiator. They also frequently object to a less serious deviancy, and overlook a more serious fault that is taking place at the same time or has taken place between the last reprimand and this.

Timing mistakes are sometimes the fault of a teacher being engrossed in other matters, but they are also often the result of a teacher being anxious not to appear too strict. For instance, if two children start to whisper, when the class should be listening to another pupil reading aloud, and a third joins them, it is a mistake of timing to wait until the third starts before reprimanding the whisperers. Even though you will not want to interrupt too often, it is a timing mistake to wait until bad behaviour has increased in seriousness before stopping it. Minor irritations of one pupil by another are frequent examples of this error in timing. One pupil pushed another's head lightly as he passed back to his seat. The second pupil then turned and dug the first pupil in the back. At that the first pupil really hit the second – and only then did the teacher consider it serious enough to reprimand him.

Timing often affects the nature of the teacher's intervention. For instance, to see something early can allow the teacher effectively to 'take action' by a gentle look, a raised finger, or a light pause in what he or she is saying. Leaving the intervention too long may force the teacher to issue a strong instruction. This can lead to things escalating, especially as this delay can mean that the teacher is unable to 'block' a pupil's instinctive attempts to avoid blame by blurting out 'I wasn't! It wasn't me!' This can open up the kind of destructive exchange that is the antithesis of the well-managed classroom.

I have found that very many of the serious incidents in classrooms that teachers cannot deal with arise out of initial errors in picking the wrong person or picking the wrong timing for the reprimand. Further, in almost all cases the teacher's error has been to leave the situation too long, thus reprimanding the second rather than the first pupil misbehaving, or the victim rather than the aggressor. In errors of target the teacher produces resentment as well as failing to stop the bad behaviour. In errors of timing it could be said that the teacher almost encourages the worse behaviour by not noticing the early stages.

If at any time you find that there is a serious situation beyond your responsibility or power, do not hesitate but immediately use whatever method the school has for gathering support. If a pupil, for instance, is grossly abusive or disobedient, do not be too proud or feel that you will weaken your position by referring the matter to a senior member of staff. (In a well-organized school it will have been made clear to you precisely whom to call and in what way. It is obviously important that the school defines roles and lines of communication clearly, and that senior staff do indeed support all their colleagues.) Also, in your Induction Year, review a number of such incidents with your Induction Tutor.

Grave breaches of discipline do occasionally happen, even with the most consistently successful teachers and even with the most co-operative pupils. You are not helping the pupil, yourself, or the school if you hesitate. The class and the individual must realize that what has happened is intolerable and that you will not tolerate it.

Therefore, send at once for a senior member of staff (usually in writing), suspend the class activity, and isolate the individual. The pupil will usually realize that retribution and apology are required. But do not hesitate.

Physical action

There might be occasions when you are tempted to hit a pupil, or otherwise use some form of physical punishment. *Don't*. However slight your action, it will do more harm than good. This includes supposedly jocular acts like hair-pulling or ear twisting. It has been well said in the past: 'Never touch a pupil in anger or affection.'

Young people properly resent any form of physical molestation. It is difficult to capture in words the deep sense of personal affront which any such action creates in most pupils. There is no halfway house. Teachers occasionally seize a pupil's collar, thinking that this is not a true physical assault. It feels it to the pupil. Furthermore, there are no nice distinctions. It is impossible in retrospect to work out exactly when you touched and what happened. If the pupil thinks the teacher used more force than he actually did, the harm to the relationship has been done and will be serious.

The only justification for physical action is to protect another person against someone's violence or themselves from their own accidental or deliberate move that could lead to danger. If possible, use a barring gesture or position rather than a grabbing one. If protecting against danger or damage requires in extremity physical action, holding both shoulders is the safest and most effective move.

You will notice that I have discussed this entirely in terms of the theme of this chapter – relationships in the classroom. That is the main reason why you should refrain from all physical punishment. In addition, however, I should remind you that to assault a pupil in any way is to lay yourself open to the possibility of discipline or prosecution by parents, and a slur on your professional record.

All that having been said, I must add that we are all human and tempers can sometimes be lost. If a time should ever come when either you are in a particularly touchy state or a pupil is extremely irritating, and you strike out, *do not cover it up*. Send at once for a senior member of staff. If no one is available, go to see your Head of Department, the Deputy Head, or your Induction Tutor as soon as the lesson is over. Explain what you did, and arrange to apologize to the family. A prompt, full, and explanatory apology is necessary, and will usually avoid troublesome and painful responses.

Humour

A joke goes a long way. Try to be light-hearted whenever you can. Try to chivvy recalcitrant pupils jokingly rather than by being indignant. 'Rule by quip', one headteacher called it. Be willing to make jokes at your own expense, and to laugh at your own foibles. Teachers' jokes do not have to be very good to be highly acceptable. I have noticed that some teachers with high ideals and considerable theoretical understanding of 'under-privileged' children take themselves, their responsibilities, and their pupils too solemnly. Their humourless indignation and sad intensity alienates their charges. I am not recommending a continuous bonanza of laughter, and certainly pupils can get tired of constant hearty jokes or tireless facetiousness. In general, through, try to be bright and modestly 'jokey'.

If you do or say anything unplanned that inadvertently makes the children laugh at you, accept the situation rapidly and gracefully. If possible, make some remark that acknowledges you have made a comic slip, join the laughter for a moment, and then quickly pick up the thread of the lesson, and reinstate the usual atmosphere.

The aim is to accept the situation and share the humour, but not to indulge yourself or them. You will not succeed in teaching if you are taken as a clown, but neither will you succeed if you are humourless and so much on your dignity that you cannot accept the pupils' laughter. Take a joke at your own expense, but do not exploit it.

Conclusion

In many ways it is lonely to be a teacher. Whatever happens, however you try, whatever intimacy you create, you will remain an adult and a teacher; your charges will remain young and pupils. It is tempting but a delusion to try to remove the barriers. This is true even in the closest situations in beyond-school activities. It is doubly so in the classroom itself. There are suitable conventions of reticence. It may well be that you will occasionally want to reveal something of your out-of-school life, but you should take care. Sometimes a fact from your own childhood or your present family life can be fairly objectively shared, for instance to express sympathy to a pupil who has lost a relative. Not only does a teacher need and deserve a private life, but once you break the normal boundary control there is no reasonable way of re-establishing it when it suits you. Furthermore, it is also an invasion of the pupils' privacy. The conventions of a certain school-teacherly distance are not the creation of proud or cold people. Rather they are the practical necessities for human contact in a continuing *professional* relationship. After all, the pupils are not of your family, and there is nothing you can do to make them so. Even if they were, there are still barriers that are mutually accepted and mutually valuable in a family. It is worth remembering how difficult parents usually find it to teach their own children. The teaching relationship can flourish precisely because it does not have the full intimacy, with all the tension that involves, of a family. As a teacher you must keep behind your barriers precisely *for the sake of the relationships*.

One of the tensions in a teacher's mind is the bringing together of one's proper ambition to establish learning progress and learning goals and one's responsibility to be also a humane and encouraging person. At a time in the twenty-first century when, for understandable reasons, there is a higher emphasis on 'goals' perhaps than there ever was in British education, it is rather easy to use learning goals and progress as a 'performance approach' with less of an emphasis on what some educational psychologists call 'mastery'. Over the years I have noticed that teachers whose conscientious anxiety to move all the pupils forward as substantially as possible without involvement with their personality often create a competitive environment that can ruin relationships and self understanding, and lead to bad behaviour. This is in no way to de-emphasize the aim of maximum learning and achievement, but to point out that it can be presented in different ways. A substantial American study of behaviour and learning targets made an important distinction between 'performance' goals and 'mastery goals', finding:

> 'Achievement goal theory suggests that the emphasis in mastery and performance goals in the classroom (the classroom goal structure) is related to students' patterns of behaviour. This theory can offer a preventative holistic approach for dealing with students' disruptive behaviour.'

In a sample of nearly four hundred pupils in Maths classrooms, the researchers found a great difference in levels of disruptive behaviour, and this collated with the observed stress on 'performance' rather than on 'mastery':

> '"Mastery" goals refer to a focus on learning, improvement, and mastering skills, whereas performance goals refer to a focus on social comparison and demonstrations of competence . . . Mastery goals have been found to be associated with the use of deep cognitive strategies, self-regulated learning, positive coping with difficulty and failure, and positive emotions towards the task and towards the school.'[13]

Although British readers will not be used to the two terms and they could cause difficulty, the key point for the craft of the classroom is that how you use the definition of targets and how you respond to your pupils' attainment has a strong relationship with disruptive behaviour.

A final word: the better things go, the better relationships will be; and then the better the lessons will go. It is the teacher's responsibility to start up this 'virtuous circle', and her or his best step is to make sure, as far as possible, that pupils keep out of trouble in the classroom. Pupils like teachers who help them develop their better selves; they dislike teachers who generate situations in which the pupils show the worse side of themselves. Run a calm, well-ordered, active classroom, in which no one is allowed to go far wrong and collaboration is the mode: you will be rewarded by growing good relationships and increased learning.

3

The classroom environment

You are lucky if you are going to have a classroom of your own. Push for it if you can, and make the most of it if you have one. (NQTs often do not have a full Tutor Group responsibility, and this reduces their 'ownership' of a classroom.) A classroom of your own means that you can far more easily and strongly create an atmosphere that reflects your character and what you have to offer the pupils who come to you; it helps you to use wall displays as teaching aids; it means that you can manage the practical supply of learning materials better, have the pupils' work easily to hand, and never have to search for anything; it means, above all, that you can use the physical environment of the room as an ally in influencing your pupils. Thus, effort taken in the care, arrangement, and maintenance of your room, especially if you enlist the help of a small number of pupils, is a valuable investment that will repay rich dividends. Put simply, not only is a well-kept and aesthetically pleasing room with functional displays an education in itself, but also pupils behave better in a room which is well organized and has individual character: the environment teaches. It is therefore appropriate that the QTS standards specifically mention the teacher's Professional Standard for this aspect of the craft of the classroom.

> 'They organize and manage the physical teaching space, tools, materials, texts and other resources safely and effectively with the help of support staff where appropriate.'[1]

The general impression which the pupil has of the room starts with the door. If there is space for a name card, and it is left to you to prepare it, do so with care, using self-adhesive letters or a carefully chosen large typeface from a word processor. If there is a window, it is best left clear, but if you are going to mount the name of your class, do so boldly, neatly, and in such a position that it is still easy to see through the window.

A clean and tidy classroom

Opening the door, the pupil's first impression is of the layout of the desks. There is something infinitely depressing about a scatter of desks and chairs with no recognizable pattern, chairs in aisles, desks at all angles. I discuss possible layouts a little later (p. 42), but I must stress the value of pleasing tidiness as the first impression a pupil receives.

She often notices the board second. Is it clean? Has it carefully prepared work on it? Or does it still bear smudged traces of earlier lessons, or, worse still, pupils' playful scrawls? I discuss the use of boards in Chapter 6. I would add here, though, that the board is boldly there to see as pupils come through the door, and it flies like an advertising flag across one side of the room, declaring it as a room of work or a room of chaos at a moment's glance.

Next, it is the general cleanliness of the room which strikes the incoming pupil. He may not comment; he may only be half consciously aware, but he will notice the floor, the ledges, and the desks. It will affect his attitude and behaviour if they are messy and if there is litter about. Make sure that the room is always tidy. Each class should be asked to clear up thoroughly before it leaves, and at the end of the day the last class should give the room a final checkover. Each pupil should be responsible for his or her area, including any neighbouring shelves or ledges and any shelves or lockers which are part of the desk. Do not allow reservoirs of litter to build up anywhere, especially under desks: it all spills out later.

Make sure that *your* sections of the room are similarly neat. Keep any piles of used books neatly and use bookends to keep your own books orderly. Teachers frequently amass miscellaneous piles of virtually abandoned books to gather chalk dust near the board. Ruthlessly clear away and chuck out regularly. In a busy teaching day you cannot afford to be confused by clutter.

Cleaning arrangements vary: some schools employ teams themselves; most have contracts with external firms, whether through the LEA or direct. The standards vary widely, but they can be excellent and you have every right to expect a thoroughly cleaned room. You can certainly help yourself by getting to know the cleaner responsible for your room. He or she deserves the thoughtfulness of your care, and you need his or her help. In some schools, chairs are put on to desks to help the cleaners. It is educationally appropriate that pupils should consider who cleans up after them, and should contribute some help at least. If you are punctilious about this help, and make sure that there is no litter on the floor, the cleaner is more likely to co-operate with you, and be able to do a better job.

Everyday maintenance

There is bound to be damage from time to time – chair backs, window catches, blinds. Do not add to the damage by putting self-adhesive tape or plastic on painted surfaces: both gloss and emulsion paint come off with the tape when it is removed and the scars remain.

Be sure you know the maintenance procedures in your school. To whom should you report damage to the fabric or furniture? Report any damage *at once*, and gently enquire about progress. Arrange for graffiti to be removed immediately. Any breakages or signs of abuse are invitations to further damage. The longer a piece of damage is left on public view, the more it contributes to the general acceptance of breakage. Anyone who has seen a heavily vandalized school will be appalled by the atmosphere of degradation. Some rooms in otherwise fairly well-kept schools also become like that. The effect on pupils of such surroundings is depressing. I strongly recommend careful efforts to maintain your room in first-rate order.

Display areas

As the pupil actually moves across the room, the effect of any display boards will strike her or him, and it is these that will be in the outskirts of her or his vision throughout the class time in the room. They form, with windows and blackboards, two of his or her learning boundaries. They are important. Most classrooms have display boards and it is wise to make good use of them. Blank boards are grey and dismal; messy boards, with the scars of past graffiti or the flaunting challenge of live graffiti, are a spur to discontent and bad behaviour. For those reasons alone, it is worth devising and maintaining lively, changing displays. More positively, however, the boards can be an active part of the teaching in a variety of ways.

You will find it easier if you roughly divide the board areas out in advance so that you can estimate approximately how often changes are required, and how much material is necessary. Have one well-kept section for the school's standing notices, whatever they may be: fire drill, lesson times, assessment schedules, list of teachers, and so on. As these will have to stay up for a whole year, they must be well pinned, preferably mounted and covered with a transparent sealing material.

Secondly, keep a small section for your own form or tutor group to display their personal, perhaps quirkish, interests: cuttings, pieces of writing, photographs, and so on.

You can then have a main central display section for some aspect of your subject which is of general interest. This should not be changed too often – you will not be able to manage it and the pupils will not have taken it in. Nor should it be left up for too long to fade and go stale. A half-termly cycle seems about right, and that requires six displays in a year. (Have the first one ready *before* term starts.) The materials for small displays can come from educational publishers, commercial posters, free handouts, press clippings, magazines, and specially prepared diagrams.

Lastly, you can mark off sections for displays of written work by each of your classes. Usually it is wise to ask each pupil discreetly if he or she would be happy to have this piece displayed. Normally these should be 'fair copies' especially prepared for display, but you may at times prefer to use first drafts. Ensure a cross-section of examples and a reasonably frequent changeover. Again, use careful display techniques.

In all four types of display, a firm grid pattern helps, and good quality labels add a great deal. Those which are likely to stand for a long time should be well prepared and protected. Finally, do not forget to *use* the displays: they can be referred to during lessons; the final minutes of a session can be given over to questions and answers in connection with them; or a class can be sent in groups to do a worksheet based on a display. Thus the displays make the room more personally yours; they add colour and interest; they have an educational function; and they show you care. They are worth the trouble.

Some teachers cultivate simple pot plants on window sills or shelves. (The success of this nicety usually depends on the willingness of the caretaking or cleaning staff to water in the holidays!) Such a pleasantness is appreciated by most pupils. The touch of colour and natural life softens the classroom, and increases pride. Of course, pupils from your own class can help with the maintenance. Other personally chosen objects or pictures to your taste can also be imported, and increase the extent of your personal touch.

Part of the aim, then, is to encourage the pupils to feel that even though they visit the room only a few times in the week, they share in the care of it. Unlike what is possible in a junior school and many middle schools, the typical secondary pattern of classes moving to teachers does not allow the full identification of pupils with 'their' room. It has, instead, to be replaced by the feeling of visiting a teacher's 'own' room. So make the room yours as completely as you can. Make it welcoming, interesting, cheerful, and workmanlike. You can make the room itself an ally of your class management.

Layout and seating

The physical layout, and especially the arrangement of the pupils' seats, is the greatest single management device. There are no hard and fast rules, but common sense has been supported by research: how the pupils are positioned influences their behaviour. For instance, a study of below-average ability Year Nine students seated in fours with pairs of two-seater tables facing found an average of 52% of the time on task. When the seating was put into rows the on-task proportion rose to 84% and then 91%. A similar experiment was tried with sixteen-year-old college students: the on-task rate rose from 64% to 75% when the chairs were changed from three rows to a single semicircle facing the lecturer.[10] The arrangement must suit the tasks intended, but some patterns positively encourage off-task behaviour. Care and ingenuity are required.

The teacher's desk

The position of the teacher's desk is worth thought. Except in some science labs, the dais has been removed from almost all rooms, and the dominant raised front-centre position abandoned. Some teachers, hoping for a close rapport with their pupils, tend to search for less and less dominating positions, perhaps shifting the desk to one side of the front, and then even down the side. I should suggest that for most purposes a front side position is probably best. The desk must be so positioned that:

- all the pupils can see the teacher when he or she is at the desk;
- the desk is clearly visible from the door as pupils enter.

Even in a relaxed modern classroom atmosphere and even in an individual research kind of lesson, the focal presence of the teacher is important. In a busy classroom you will see pupils' eyes flick up to where they expect to see the teacher. Some of the looks will be from pupils wondering momentarily whether to do something silly or not. Others will be from pupils who are deep in their work but want some kind of reassurance. The stable figure of the teacher in a known position in the room is a comforting influence for the collaborative enterprise. This position, therefore, does need to be a focal point.

Secondly, your desk will be where you lay out what *you* need for the lesson. Occasionally, a teacher's overuse of the instruction 'Put it on my desk' can lead to a muddle of piles that confuses your work. Spare paper for the pupils can be in a position convenient for their movement to it, but your books, class list, notes, pens, handbag, and anything you might want whilst talking to the class or helping an individual must be conveniently laid out. The teacher's desk is normally the best place for all this, and so it must be near your normal focal position. I have seen teachers placing their desk in an out-of-the-way position, and then finding that they have difficulty dodging back and forth.

Thirdly, if you wish to give a great deal of individual tuition you will probably find this done best at your own desk, with a pupil sitting to one side. (I find this immensely more effective than dodging about the room, crouching or bending to help individuals, as I describe later on pp. 91–2.) This means, again, that your desk must be placed in a focal position, so that you can still influence the room whilst helping individuals; that there must be sufficient space by your desk for a pupil's chair; and that there must be reasonably easy access to and from the desk.

For all these reasons the teacher is usually much happier in a room where she or he has a desk or table which is easy to get at and round; is adjacent to the best focal position for board work and whole-class presentation; and is in a pleasant position for when the teacher is quietly helping an individual pupil.

Pupils' layout

How do you want the pupils' tables or desks laid out? There is rarely an ideal layout in a normal-sized classroom, but the search for an optimum layout is worthwhile. The basic difficulty is to arrange the furniture so that each pupil can have both the degree of privacy necessary for the majority of work, and the possibility of co-operative groupings at other times. A second difficulty is to arrange the desks so that each pupil has as much space as possible, and yet there is sufficient space for movement around the class. Equal spacing, for instance, suits the first aim, and allows each pupil the maximum elbow room. However, by losing all the circulation space, it creates congestion when the teacher or a pupil needs to move around the room. Circulation space must be kept. It is often forgotten that if there is to be a great deal of individual work this space is even more important: the individual assignment cards used in some parts of courses all presume a steady flow of pupils moving to pick up the next card, check a completed card, or gather new materials. The regulation aisles, which usually have no cross connection without pushing against chair backs, are inadequate.

Perhaps the greatest technical problem is to find an optimum pattern that allows the different activities from individual writing to small-group work, especially when the basic furniture is two-seater desks. A number of patterns are possible even so: a regular chequer-board rectangular pattern; a single horseshoe, which makes the desks or tables into a continuous inward-facing row; island blocks, with tables grouped for pupils to face inwards. If you do not have exclusive use of a room, to devise eccentric arrangements is unfair on your colleagues, of course. All the users have to agree.

Where do pupils sit?

Careful thought should be given in advance to what line you are going to take about the pupils' regular positions at desks, tables, lab benches, or other work-benches. You cannot dither as your pupils first arrive, nor can you easily change your mind from lesson to lesson. In particular, it is virtually impossible to change after a number of sessions in which there has been free pupil choice. You must take the decision in advance, and then keep to it for at least a considerable run of time.

The issue is simple to define: are the best interests of the pupils served by allowing them to choose their own normal positions, or is there anything to be gained by your determining the arrangements yourself? Before deciding, it is worth a careful exploration of the often contradictory attitudes that lie behind the arguments on both sides.

At first glance it seems more generous, more in tune with encouraging pupil autonomy, and more likely to gain the goodwill of the pupils if you allow them to find their own places. Certainly you would expect post-sixteen students to settle their own seating, but how far down the age range would you go? And what characteristic is it that would lead you to make the decision? It is worth remembering the different situations and not merely the different ages: older students frequently meet in a room with spare seats, for a subject which they have chosen, and in a much smaller group than a younger class. In other words, it is not merely age that should be taken into account but the entire pattern of the activity.

A full class of, say, 30 pupils coming into a room with which they are not familiar and being left to themselves is interesting to observe. A few come in first and settle in a group by the window; a bunch of three or four dash for the back and ensconce themselves with a defiant air of territorial possession; friends try to keep together; a few nervous children find it difficult to settle as the odd seats apparently left over prove to be reserved for friends. At the end you usually find a quiet boy desperately trying to avoid the only seat, which is in fact next to a girl, whereas the rest of the class are sexually segregated. Undirected, most pupils in the early and middle secondary years sit next to a friend of the same sex. As a teacher you find yourself atmospherically excluded from various of the groups which have formed, and you soon realize that you have neither a 'class' nor a series of individuals but a number of factions of different strengths and degrees of unity to contend with.

It could be argued, and frequently is, that this kind of peer-group-determined seating is precisely what is best for the pupils, for it will encourage co-operation and maintain the favourable attitude of the pupils.

I am by no means certain that justice, pleasantness, or learning effectiveness are on the side of allowing the pupils to choose their seating arrangements. In the first place, the teacher must be the leader of the classroom: her will power must be sufficient to make things work. By making the first set of decisions about seating, she is clearly stating that this is her room, and that things will be run her way. (There will be ample opportunity later for the pupils to exercise their influence.) For the teacher to start the year by organizing the seating is to start as she intends to go on – as the leader.

Secondly, I'm not at all sure that the apparent friendship groups that determine the seating when a free-for-all is allowed are *always* the most beneficial ones for the pupils. Some are more *power* groups than friendship groups, and these are not necessarily appreciated equally throughout the class by all the pupils. As so often happens, the vociferous few may well have their demands met at the expense of the general good. The powerful block that this system allows to flourish almost inevitably draws the teacher's time and care, both in class teaching and individual work, from the remainder of the class. Time and time again I have seen teachers allow, even encourage, such groups to grow in the interest of fairness, freedom, and gaining goodwill, only to find the class as a whole is unmanageable because of an obstreperous caucus which dominates the room and is impossible to satisfy or quieten. Often these dominant groups are all boys, and some join only to build or keep their peer-group image: they feel they *have* to be part of the group. Directly focusing on the group as a whole is often counter-productive, as they pull together and strengthen their bonds. It is usually best to speak to individuals away from the group, and to find reasons for reseating some of them, such as special tasks.

Thirdly, I am not at all sure that 'friends' need each other or are always good for each other in the work of classroom assignments. Whatever the class activity – a mixed-attainment class coping with worksheets, pairs co-operating, small group work, or the whole class listening to a presentation – a proportion of your pupils is going to be easily distracted. The distractors will usually be their friends. Some pupils spend so much time in each other's company in homes, street, and playground that they just cannot resist teasing each other, joking, and talking. It is harmless, pleasant, but distracting. There is no hardship in expecting these close friends to work for a double period in other groupings – they get hours of each other's company. It is in no way 'unreal' or 'artificial', for in most jobs they will have to work independently of best friends. Indeed, it is a necessary preparation for all kinds of work to learn to work quietly on your own.

It is in fact a truism that some pupils need protecting *from* their friends, so that they can be more genuinely themselves. Indeed, the art of a successful student is to be alone without being lonely. This needs to be taught and learned, and pupils released from what Alec Dickson, the founder of Community Service Volunteers, appropriately called 'the prison of the peer group'. One small-scale study[10] raised the on-task proportion of time of a Year Nine class from 76% to 91% after changing the seating from self-chosen same-sex positions to compulsory mixed sex ones.

Fourthly, 'individualized' teaching requires the teaching of individuals when there is not a real need for a group togetherness. Teachers commonly stress their wish to teach individuals. Often, however, they allow virtually impenetrable small groups to bring their ring-fenced relationships into the classroom. Thus the teacher is unable to develop a truly individual approach to Naheed as she is always part of the Siamese twin 'Naheed and Sumitra'. Whilst it is certainly true that her closeness to Sumitra is part of her and to be respected, it is also true that the teacher will never get near to the real Naheed until he can prise them apart and get her on her own. Then he will find unexpected sides to her character. Whilst the pair are performing as a pair, only those parts of their characters which overlap are allowed by either of them to surface. The rest is deliberately hidden. Those hidden parts need teaching also, and are often more teachable than the joint features of the 'Naheed and Sumitra' pair. It shows no real respect for the individuals Naheed and Sumitra to let them remain together, and it tends to deny them both communication with the teacher, and even with the other members of the class.

Fifthly, supposedly free choice (it is not, after all, free for many of the pupils) almost inevitably leads to arguments in subsequent lessons when two or three pupils have decided to vary their seats; a few others, finding 'their' seats taken, obligingly search out alternatives; and a chain of moves is necessary as the pupils gradually fill the room. Somewhere along the line, however, a pupil sticks, insists on 'his' own place, and refuses the empty seat. At that point there is a ripple of arguments that is difficult or impossible for any teacher to sort out. As such an arrangement has invested no especial authority in any particular pattern of seats, and as each period has had some slight variation, there is no clear scheme or agreed precedent to refer to. As the pupils themselves established all the variations, there is no authority to arbitrate. The lesson founders before it starts in a welter of pointless arguing. In the end the teacher finds she is absolutely obliged to dictate some shifts and reseatings. She has lost the goodwill, wasted time, and has the unenviable task of starting a lesson amongst sulks. The paradox is that the earlier apparent freedom leads to frequent reimpositions of the teacher's will. There is not time in a school day or space in a school classroom for this kind of difficulty.

Sixthly, there will sometimes be specific pedagogic reasons for certain seating requirements, of which the most obvious are physical difficulties (such as poor eyesight or a movement disability) or an EAL pupil who will have a specialist teacher working alongside her or him sometimes.

Finally, there is the teacher's need to know without a moment's thought exactly where each pupil is working. Especially with large classes, this is possible only if each pupil works in the same position period after period. Then the teacher absorbs the pattern into his subconscious, and can turn to a pupil straightaway.

For these seven reasons, then, I should strongly recommend that the initial seating of a class is done by the teacher and to a plan devised by him or her. In a science laboratory or D&T workshop this may involve two sets of positions: those for central explanation and those for individual or small-group activity and experiment.

Making a seating plan

Prepare a sketch plan of the work positions available in your room. Make copies of this if you like – sufficient for two or so for each of your classes. Then study your class list and what you know of each pupil before deciding on your arrangement. An alphabetical sequence is the obvious arbitrary decision that does not raise any challengeable points. It also has the added practical advantage, for which you will be grateful week after week, that it follows the normal order of registers, school lists, and your own mark-book, and this helps your remembering of their names. Notice, however, that even the apparently inflexible alphabetical order offers you some helpful variations. If you are teaching in a mixed school, for instance, it used to be normal to list girls first and then boys. Now it is more usual to produce a single alphabetical list, boys and girls together in their correct alphabetical position, as it is preferable for reasons of gender equity. I prefer this for seating as most misbehaviour in class results from the interaction of pupils of the same sex. This scheme frequently puts a boy next to a girl. Of course, you can achieve this even more rigorously by interspersing boy/girl with two separate alphabetical sequences, but this makes the listing more complicated, and is not so simple to explain to the class.

If you are lucky enough to have slightly fewer pupils in your teaching group than there are actual seats or work-bench spaces in your room, I strongly recommend that you exploit the spare seats as buffers to improve the psychological separation of pupils or groups. It is pointless to allow a block of four empty seats when other sectors of the room are crowded. Instead, distribute the spare seats as you judge best. It might be wise with one class to keep the back row, the troublemaker's instinctive chair-swinging row, empty. In another class you may distribute the empty seats here and there, merely to thin the seating out. You may use your knowledge of the pupils in another class to decide that Gary or Elaine is best left sitting in isolation. After all, in a great deal of learning activity a psychological barrier between individuals is valuable – I would not want someone nudging me or breathing down my neck whilst I was drafting this chapter. You would find it harder to read the chapter if your best friend were right next to you, constantly asking you to borrow your pen, pencil, ruler, and so on.

In small-group work, you may occasionally require homogeneous sub-grouping, in which case you clearly must organize the groups yourself. You may, on the other hand, want pairs or groups to be mixed also, in which case your influence is equally necessary. The fluidity of varying working groups implies the need for the control that comes only from controlled seating. The seating plan, then, is a method of assisting the psychological insulation of crowded pupils, and can sometimes be subtly manipulated to separate certain individuals or to leave others entirely on their own.

Using the seating plan

Have your seating arrangement decided and noted down in advance. Prepare a sketch plan of the work positions available, and run off one or two blanks for each class. Have one in your hand when you first greet the incoming class. A second copy is useful as the first pupil who arrives can be issued with it and stationed on the far side of the room to help with the directions: it is much better to get pupils straight to the seats you have chosen, rather than to have to evict them. That does cause resentment. If you feel it is better to seat them rapidly any old how, make the pupils fill the seats up from the front as they come in. Do not let the choosing process start, and then disappoint the early squatters. When the seats are full, go round the desks calling out the names of the permanent tenants, asking each dispossessed pupil to rise and stand at the front until his or her name is called for a seat. You will find that this method of reseating works quite well.

Post one copy of the seating plan on the notice board for checking up if necessary at the start of the next lesson, and paste the other copy clearly in your class register. You will find this very convenient, as it allows you to identify the pupils by name rapidly. You may also like to have each pupil note the position of his or her desk in a workbook on the first occasion, to help memorize it for the next lesson.

There will be many occasions when you reorganize for special purposes, for instance research assignments practising information skills in the library, using ICT equipment, discussions in a tutorial period, visits out of school for local studies. In all such cases the earlier care over seating arrangements will have benefited the ability of your pupils to work successfully in the most appropriate groups. Care over initial seating contributes more than any other single action to the management of the class in subsequent weeks.

Conclusion

It would be fair to say that the physical impression of the classroom can be an ally or an enemy in teaching, and part of the craft of the classroom is to *use* the room itself. Its arrangement, displays, atmosphere, and practical details will contribute to the class management, the learning, the relationships, and the pleasure of working together collaboratively. The care of the room and the effectiveness of the displays speaks to the pupils and helps your relationships and your teaching.

The Professional Standard (3.3.8) quoted on p. 38 is expanded in the TTA's *Handbook of Guidance* in terms which are essential but not complete:

> 'Classrooms are busy and active places where both pupils and teachers need to use a range of resources safely and effectively. In order to be able to use the most effective teaching strategies and provide a productive and safe

learning environment, teachers use teaching space and resources flexibly.'[6]

We need to go further than that and also take into account the aesthetic and atmospheric aspects: attitude, interest, involvement, and inter-personal relationships gain from a suitable environment. An interesting way of considering the overall environment of the classroom has been made by teacher-trainers and researchers who have used ideas from the study of ecology further to understand the overall classroom environment. The idea of an 'ecosystem' is that all aspects are interlinked so that damage to or neglect of one inevitably affects the whole system to a considerable extent. The classroom is indeed an 'ecosystem', and an eye for detail and care for each aspect and their interface brings a significant strength to the educational life of the pupils in the classroom.

4

Records and registers

Teachers traditionally despise 'paperwork', but good record-keeping is essential both to the success of an individual teacher's work and to the relationship between his work and that of other colleagues. It is not on the whole a retrospective chore required by external forces. Rather, records facilitate the analytic heart of teaching, as well as enabling professional collaboration, working towards external assessment, and preparing for reporting to parents. Indeed, the National Record of Achievements required for students at the end of Year Eleven are best seen as a culmination of the earlier years of assessment and record-keeping. As a tutor and as a course teacher, you will find the highest ideals of pastoral care are built on the most mundane record-keeping. Similarly, your analysis of a pupil's growth in skills and understanding in the courses you teach grows out of your records.

A major part of the record-keeping is making good use of the pupils' previous and current different forms of assessment. Many teachers feel over-burdened by the twenty-first century use of assessment to judge teachers and schools. There have been times in the past when we have under-used assessment – for instance, not diagnosing dyslexia as early as can be helpful, or not enabling the pupil to understand her or his strengths and difficulties. One of the United Kingdom's leading educational specialists in the use of assessment is Mary James of the Cambridge University Department of Education. She sums up:

> 'The principal idea is that assessment processes should be put to work for school improvement by assisting schools and teachers in helping students to learn, thereby increasing their achievements.'[14]

53

Assessments are there to support you as a teacher. Of course, measurements can be made of only certain aspects, and these will not always be the most important aspects of personal, social, moral, intellectual, physical, and cultural growth. It is worth helping your pupils understand that, as I have come to put it: 'A test tests only what a test tests.' For instance, in reading neither tenacity nor love of reading can be measured, although they are both important qualities. However, the teacher's work with her or his pupils can be helped by making good use of the assessment that is available. The essence is neither to push forms of assessment to one side nor to base too much on one assessment. The TTA put this well in the requirement that those awarded QTS 'must demonstrate':

> 'They make appropriate use of a range of monitoring and assessment strategies to evaluate pupils' progress towards planned learning objectives, and use this information to improve their own planning and teaching.'[1]

Thus, part of the craft of the classroom is to make use of records and registers as a sensitive and valuable tool to assist you with your support of your pupils.

Your register or mark-book

What is commonly called a 'mark-book' or 'register' is in fact your professional, central, portable record system, by which you monitor and record your many pupils' attendance, work, progress, and a wide range of other facts. Do not over-trust your memory. A secondary teacher may have a caseload of between 150 and 300 pupils for whom he or she is responsible in courses and tutorials. No one's memory can hold all that is required for the teaching of so many people without the aid of detailed records.

Electronic registration is very widely used and adds the immense advantage of instantaneous checking with the early morning's attendance of a pupil not in a lesson later in the day. If you are lucky enough to be in a school with such a scheme, realize that it reduces a huge amount of pen and paper work, has an exponential inter-staff communication strength, and most importantly, facilitates 'cross-checking' during the day and across the week.

Although the primary purpose of full records is for the teacher to help himself with his teaching, it is also worth remembering the inevitable absences. If a teacher is away ill and an absence-cover teacher has to take over his or her lessons, the records are essential. Teachers should ask themselves just how comprehensive and effective their records would be if another teacher tried to continue to teach the classes in his or her absence.

Uses for the records

There are five main uses for these records:

The list of pupils for whom you are responsible

When you are teaching the school's standard registration units ('forms', 'classes', or 'tutor groups'), you will normally take these lists off the school's master lists. If, on the other hand, you are teaching 'sets' (that is, groupings formulated only for the one subject course, for instance in GCSE options), you must get these lists from your Head of Department. Either way, be accurate in transferring the names to your records, and let the pupils know clearly that you have such a list. (Do not accept into your class pupils who are not on your list! In large schools obliging teachers have been known to accept pupils who turned up to a lesson, and to put their names at the foot of the list. Weeks later it is discovered that these pupils ought to be somewhere else!)

Leave space alongside each pupil's name for such basic information such as the name of his Tutor (if yours is a mixed set), medical information, and so on. It is worth leaving a few vertical columns blank alongside the list of names. It is especially important to have a ready reminder of each pupil's Tutor, whom you will often wish to inform or consult.

Attendance at lessons

It is an absolute obligation to check during each lesson which pupils are present and which are absent from your room. It is easiest if you date the head of each column so that there is a column for each session at which you will meet in the term. If you put a heavier rule after each week's columns it will be easier to find your place. This kind of advance preparation of the mark-book is amply repaid by the time saved when you are actually in the classroom coping with the pupils. It is hopeless to write in names *then*, and even heading columns wastes time.

Some time during each lesson, enter those present and absent. It is not necessary, nor is it normally wise, to actually 'call' the register aloud unless you do not know the pupils' names well enough for a visual check. It is certainly not good practice to do so at the start of a lesson, as this requires you to hold the attention of the class and control their behaviour for a list of names, an unnecessarily difficult job and boring for the pupils. However, it is most important that the pupils know that you *do* check the attendance carefully and regularly, for there is plenty of evidence that in areas where truancy is attractive and fairly common, pupils absent themselves not so much from teachers or lessons they do not like as teacher who they know do not make careful checks (this is helpfully termed 'Post-Registration Truancy'[9]). Thus, in the early days the list of names can be called aloud, whilst the pupils are working, and throughout the year you should demonstrate that you are checking regularly.

Each school will have its own procedures to help you ascertain whether those absent from your lessons are genuinely absent from school or not. In some schools you will be expected to check with lists of absentees posted on a central notice board; in others, you will have to check with the main class register; and in others, there will be routine chits that you are expected to fill up and send to the Head of Year, Head of House, or office. More and more schools use the powerfully effective electronic registration systems. Be punctilious about these procedures, and *let the pupils know that you do this checking as a matter of course.*

Records of work completed

The sequence of attempted assignments a student works in your class is a history of her or his learning development, and your record of this is necessary for your diagnoses, feedback, professional collaboration, statutory assessment, and reporting to parents. You must know what your pupils have accomplished and where their difficulties lie. This leads to and involves target-setting, even though not all aspects of future achievement are amenable to measurable targets. Schools have different policies on target-setting and within that different subject courses and the tutorial session obviously vary in the possibilities and methods that really suit. Yet a key aspect of all teaching is recording attainment and setting targets. This use of records for forward planning is an important aspect of developing your pupils' knowledge, skills, and attitudes.

Obviously your recording grows out of the curriculum policy that led to the assignment: what were the specific learning objectives, but at the same time what whole-school policies are relevant (for instance, literacy)? 'Marking' is one of those very widely used words from the technical vocabulary of schools, but the range of activities it encompasses is often overlooked. In most cases your written comments engaging with the pupil's ideas and solutions are the most important task: you are running, as it were, a seminar in writing. Sometimes your summary will be only in words, but an overall grade in numbers or letters is usual, both as a simple feedback to the pupil, her parents, and her tutor, but also for your ease of recording.

Your department should have a broad but flexible policy which will guide you. Many schools have an agreed and moderated grading system, often derived from externally validated grading scales as Standard Assessment statutory grades; others leave nomenclature, scales, referencing, and moderation to the course departments. For the sake of feedback to students and their families, internal professional discussions, and contributions to building up a student profile, referencing onto a single scale is decidedly preferable. There can be great misunderstandings if each teacher uses an idiosyncratic scale.

The Levels of Attainment of the National Curriculum offer a set of criteria which can be used to record achievements. Certainly a school's assessment policy should incorporate, but be wider than, national statutory requirements. Within it there should not be a sharp disjunction between regular class assessment and external requirements.

GCSE assessment involves a specific judgement and mark-weighting based on the candidate's written grammar and spelling, as accuracy of expression is important. However, some of the school-teaching traditions of earlier decades have embodied another stance: that pupils struggling to think out issues in a subject course, whether Science or History, should not be constrained by concerns over correctness of expression. Whilst a proper balance between those two stances is difficult to achieve, your assessing and recording, whatever subject courses you teach, should take the quality and correctness of written expression into account. It is not fair for pupils and their parents to discover only in the pre-examination run-up that there are significant weaknesses of expression.

Each subject course in the secondary school will require a slightly different recording system, but basically the teacher needs to note each step or item of work completed. When the entire class is expected to do each exercise or piece of writing simultaneously, and to finish on the same occasion, the recording of this is fairly easy. Even with an ever-increasing variety of assignments, this work pattern is still very common, and is likely to remain so.

There are two basic ways of recording the items of work done: a vertical column can identify the *dates* of the work sessions, in class or at home, if all the pupils are doing the same piece of work; the horizontal line against the pupil's name indicates satisfactory completion by a tick, or can be used for a grade or 'mark'.

If the pupils are working on different assignments, such as different stages of a work-card scheme or different self-chosen pieces of writing, the horizontal line indicates briefly the title or number of the piece of work. Obviously, in this case, a greater horizontal width is required, and two or three vertical columns are best used for each session. Alternatively, if the pupils are expected to work methodically, but at their own individual paces, through a sequence of assignments, the *vertical* columns can be used to identify the assignments, and the pupils' horizontal lines the dates on which each assignment is completed. Grades can easily be incorporated into this dating system.

There is an obvious need to join together the second function – attendance – with this third function – work completed. With the number of classes and the normal pattern of a secondary school timetable, you will find it impossible to remember with certainty who completed what when. I have heard interminable arguments between a well-meaning teacher and devious pupils about whether a piece of work from a week or two back should have been done or not:

'But I was absent, Miss.'
'Not on the day we did that piece of work.'
'Yes, I was. Don't you remember, Miss, 'cos when I came back ...'

And so it goes on. Your records need to be clear enough to avoid all arguments. Linking the printed attendance records from a school's electronic registration system with your record of work completed can be difficult. One possible method is to use separate pages for work and attendance. In that case you need to check back when there is doubt. Alternatively, you can put the pupils' names only on *every other* horizontal line, using the first horizontal line for absent/present signs, and the second one for work records, thus:

	10 Sept	12 Sept	14 Sept	17 Sept	19 Sept	21 Sept
JAMILA BEGUM	✓	✓	✓	✓	✓	✓
	6	6	7		7	8
CLODETH BROWN	A	✓	✓	✓	✓	✓
		8	5		6	4
LORRAINE CLARKE	✓	✓	A	A	✓	✓
	4	5		3	3	
. . . .						
. . . .						
	Exercise 3	Research	Diagrams		Test	Story

Either way, I recommend a clear code system to remind you of the work situation. For every work session when something should have been committed to paper (whether a homework session or a class session), there are five possibilities. I recommend that you decide on a sign for each square in your mark-book that will later tell you immediately and unambiguously what happened. You will find this most helpful when you read through the pupils' work at home later, and when you hand it back:

The pupil hands in completed work (leaving space for
grade later):   ✓

The pupil was absent, and did not do the work: A

The pupil was absent when the work should have been
handed in, but not when it should have been done (this
especially applies to homework) (again, space left for
grade later):   a

The pupil did not hand anything in, and needs chasing: o

The pupil present and worked, but did not complete,
and more time is agreed: —

Obviously there are unnumerable variations in ways of using a gridded mark-book to keep tabs on the flow of work. Be clear, consistent, and careful, and you will remove almost all the classroom arguments that sour relationships and take time. Records are not anti-creative: they are the servants of caring teaching, serving not only towards external assessment, but also acting as feedback to your teaching for future planning. There are no absolutely 'correct' methods, but it is very practicable to study the records of colleagues and devise your own in the light of their practices.

Special care is required with long research studies or extended pieces of writing: it is easy to lose track of the overall progress. If after a number of weeks the pupil does not complete and hands in a very skimpy piece, it is too late to intervene.

Record of books issued

In a later section (on p. 78) I discuss ways of handing out books, apparatus, and worksheets for a single lesson. Books issued to be taken away from the room, however, must be recorded, and this is a further function of the mark-book.

Most subjects use sets of printed books at least some of the time; indeed, for all the emphasis on other kinds of resources, many subjects depend on every pupil having a book to hand, especially to re-read and study for homework assignments. The teacher must establish a routine which is as helpful as possible in making sure that there is no confusion over these books.

Their handling can be divided into two categories: books issued for a single session only, and books issued for the pupil to take away for a short or long period. The first category can be thought of in exactly the same way as apparatus and equipment issued for use during a period, and I therefore give advice in the section on p. 78. Books to be taken away, however, require a different approach. It must be simple, and must be carried out precisely and briskly.

Your school or department may well have a system. If so, you will obviously use it. If not, I recommend the following. Make sure in advance that the set of books is clearly serial numbered from one upwards. This is best done with a specially prepared self-inking stamp, and many departments prepare these:

> **Sir Henry Wood School**
> **Golder Grove, Colchester**
> **HISTORY DEPARTMENT**
> **Set No:** *4a*
> **Copy Number:** *5*

Other departments have very large self-inking numbered stamps that can be applied to the top of the page edges of the closed book. I find this a less satisfactory method on its own, but it is very clear in a pile of books. If no provision has been made for you, simply number each copy boldly and firmly, perhaps in a coloured ink, in precisely the same place in each copy, perhaps the bottom right-hand corner of the front inside cover. Tell the pupils clearly that each copy is numbered and that you will be keeping a record of the number of each copy in your class list, so that you will know exactly who has which copy.

I recommend that, if possible, you actually issue the copies whilst the class are busy with some other work. Do not go round with the full pile of books first, and then gather the numbers. Call each pupil to you one by one (or visit each pupil's desk), hand over the copy yourself, show the number, and let the pupil see that it is entered in the list against his or her name. In addition, of course, each pupil should write his or her name neatly and clearly in the book, using the official school label if there is one.

It is difficult for pupils to remember an irregular requirement for bringing books to lessons, and spontaneous decisions like 'Oh ... and I'd like you to bring your atlas to tomorrow's lesson' are almost always a failure: some do not hear, many forget, a few who come tomorrow are away today, and others have lost their atlas because you use it so rarely. The regular bringing of a clearly stated number of books is easier for all. (If there is a book you use only rarely, then you may prefer to issue it, as discussed on p. 78, only for the necessary periods.) Insist on this routine, and make a fuss about it in the early weeks. Keep the Form Teacher or Tutor informed of any failures. Build up the habit and give lavish praise when it is established. It is perfectly reasonable that your lesson should depend on books and other printed material: only the creation of a routine will ensure that the majority bring them.

Comments on the pupils

You should certainly exercise the focusing discipline of going through your class lists once a term and asking yourself how each pupil has been getting on, and recording a comment. This may be required for external reports, as a contribution towards profiling or target-setting, or for internal records. If not, do it for your own benefit. Either way, the mark-book is an easy place, although you may prefer to use a sheet of paper in the pupil's folder, which I mention on p. 74. If you use the mark-book, allow a full double-page spread, cut back so that it aligns with your pupil list.

Further suggestions

Before we leave mark-*books*, it is worth mentioning that although the single book, which has now become the storehouse for so much information about each of your pupils, is very convenient indeed, there are other possible formats. For instance, a double-pocket folder for a single class can have in the centre fold sufficient gridded mark-book pages for the class. The pupils' current work or file paper can be kept in one pocket, and examples of worksheets, and so on, in the other. There is then a compendium for the class with everything that is needed in it. Various forms of portable computers with communication for central records are also widely used.

Subjective comments on aspects of each pupil's attitude, skills, and achievement should be recorded alongside any more objective grades or scores. The cumulative value of these for your own work, for the overview by the school of the pupil, and for the build-up to national assessment is very great indeed.

Attendance registers

The formal attendance register of the tutor group is of especial importance, as a diagnostic tool, a legal document (which may have to be produced as evidence in the case of attendance prosecution), and for the statutorily required attendance figures for individual parents and aggregation for school publication.

All schools have their standard registers, with detailed instructions. These may be issued by the LEA or devised by the school, whether it is a 'Foundation School' or LEA 'Community' school. As I said on p. 56, a very large number now use the extremely helpful electronic systems.

If you have pastoral responsibility as a Tutor or Form Teacher, you must see the formal attendance register not as some piece of routine bureaucracy, but as a useful way of helping you to help the pupils and their families. In the first place, you must know who is and is not in school, and the school must inform the parents of any absences by whatever convenient but certain procedure it has devised. This is not only a legal necessity but a professional duty: the parent who has seen the child off to school must be informed if he or she has not arrived. A clear distinction between 'authorized' and 'unauthorized' absences will be defined by the school following statutory requirements and must be punctiliously adhered to.

Secondly, the register is used as a clear record of all notes about absences, dental appointment cards, and the like received about pupils, and all information notes about attendance sent to the parents. In many, perhaps most, cases this information serves merely as a running check that you have indeed received the necessary explanatory notes. In cases of difficulty, however, you will find that meticulous record-keeping proves invaluable time and again when the problem is being reviewed, either by you as Tutor or by senior pastoral staff. When the school staff need to talk over attendance problems with parents, the existence of an accurate register, with details of notes and action taken, is vital.

Thirdly, the register records lateness. The normal procedure is to make a circle if the pupil is not present at the official registration time, and insert an 'L' if he or she arrives later. You should regard lateness as an aspect of attendance, as, indeed, does the law: the courts regard continuous lateness as an attendance failure. The register needs to be accurate, parents need to be informed, and action taken must be noted.

The fourth point about the register is that, if used sensitively and carefully, it is a remarkably effective diagnostic device. You can see if worrying patterns are building up. Look out for the pattern of absence: the odd half-days are the most worrying. When do they come? Is there any consistent pattern that relates to the time of the week (for example, Monday a.m., Friday p.m.), or the lesson timetable (Does Mary tend to miss Maths?), or other pupils' absences (Are two boys truanting together?). Study your register weekly and look *back* over the year for each pupil. Always make sure parents know of *every* absence or lateness, but also watch if the incidence of either is above average or abnormally patterned. You may then spot difficulties at home, at school, or within the pupil.

The tutor group register is also useful to you as a course teacher. You can check your pupils' attendance of your classes against the rest of their week – indeed, sometimes spot 'post-registration truancy': the pupil is in school, but not at your lesson. This has been shown by sample research studies to be far more common than is widely recognized. Significantly, it varies not only between schools but between subject courses in schools: the pupils with truancy tendencies indulge their post-registration truancy with the teachers they know have the less efficient attendance checks and records.

Internal notes

Throughout your teaching there will be a need to inform or consult colleagues about the pupils whom you teach. Perhaps in a very small school it is possible to hold all the needs for communication in your head. In most schools, though, notes are necessary. They also have the advantage of being able to be filed if necessary, and they allow the recipient to consider the matter you have raised at leisure. There is little more infuriating in a large school than a stream of corridor remarks in which, between your classroom and the staffroom cup of tea, three or four teachers throw out important tit-bits of information, most of which you may forget to act on, as no mind can take in that kind of casual barrage.

It is a good idea to have a notepad always with your mark-book, or a supply of slips inside it, so that you can write out notes or queries to colleagues as the points come to you in your lesson, and you can then post them in staffroom pigeonholes at the end of the session. I am not suggesting that paperwork can be or should be a substitute for personal discussion, but I am stressing that you will *never* have all the conversations about your pupils that you would like, and that you should therefore be willing to use notes as a starting point.

Conclusion

Pupils' files are legally open to their guardians or parents. Whilst any descriptions of pupils should be frank, they should not slip into indignant exaggeration. You could subsequently be challenged, and your colleagues will find an accurate note of events more helpful than a view of the pupil's character.

Finally, for all these points the positive, praising note is as valuable or more so than the criticism, though well gauged criticisms are necessary and can be enabling. Try to keep a realistic balance.

As a teacher you will find accurate and comprehensive recording valuable for yourself and for the wider work of the school – both in the short and the longer term. It will also contribute to your report writing for families. The United Kingdom used to be well behind other countries in the usefulness of school reports. Towards the end of the last century there was a substantial improvement. Good oral and written reports require good record-keeping. It was a major step when the TTA included as an integral requirement for skill in communication with families for QTS, requiring that:

> 'They can communicate sensitively and effectively with parents and carers, recognizing their roles in pupils' learning, and their rights, responsibilities and interests in this.'[1]

Accurate, clear, and vivid recording is an essential part of this.

5

Conventions and routines

Every kind of room, from a pub bar to a railway compartment, from a cinema to a snack bar, has to have its own conventions of behaviour if the central activity is to take place satisfactorily, and if the people in it are to manage not to offend or interfere with one another. In a public room with a person-to-floor-space density of $8\frac{1}{2}$ square feet per person, one door of 3'6" wide, much necessary furniture, and books and papers galore, a set of well-understood conventions is essential for everyone's benefit. Furthermore, pupils are compelled by law to come to school and the least we can do is to create a situation in which each pupil feels comfortable and that his or her time has been profitably spent. Achieving this involves creating a set of conventions for the classroom that are, in very many ways, different from those of the home.

The teacher is responsible for creating and sustaining these conventions, and must not feel hesitant about doing so. They have to be embodied in classroom routines. A convention is a way of economizing on decision-making energy. Just as the conventional greeting of 'Good morning!' avoids the need to think up a form of words to initiate each conversation, so conventions of classroom action avoid dozens of daily decisions. Some conventions may not look too sturdy when examined in other lights and on other occasions; nevertheless they may be immensely valuable in their place. All this is to argue for the value of classroom routines lightly applied, for they assist class management, permit the growth of close relationships, and allow learning to flourish.

Receiving the class

The majority of secondary teachers are based in their own rooms for most of their teaching time. I have spoken in Chapter 3 of the value of maintaining your classroom pleasantly and efficiently. I gave there a number of reasons for this: one of them, of course, is the psychological value of receiving the pupils into your own territory and a place which is not merely an institutional convenience but also has a definite character. However, whether it is your room or just one you use for a particular session each week, the following advice applies.

Be in the room first if at all possible. Unpack and lay out your personal papers and books rapidly and neatly, so that when the pupils have arrived, anything you want is to hand, and you do not have to dive into your bag or fumble through a pile of belongings. Check quickly that the room is in order, the board clean, chalk or board pens ready, and any necessary worksheets or books are there. This preliminary early settling in is very helpful. Try very hard to fit it in, even if it means leaving the staffroom chat a little earlier than the old hands. It will be worth it to be first in the room.

Where should you be when the first pupils arrive? Well, obviously there is no one correct place. However, do not be lost in the far corner or in a tangle in a stock cupboard. Be seen to be the receiving host, as it were. Be in a focal point to encourage the first pupils to go straight to their first activity. Centre-front is clearly one very good position. My own preference, however, is to stand in the doorway, back against the door jamb, facing down the classroom, and at the same time down the corridor outside. (If most teachers were thus positioned at their doors, many of the problems of noisy corridors would be solved.) In this position you can greet each pupil or group of pupils as they arrive, and direct them to their first activity. As each passes you, it is possible to put in a personal word to many of them. Private jokes, reminders, enquiries, warnings, and encouragement can all be easily fitted in. You have combined efficient supervision with warm personal relationships – and given instructions for the first activity.

The start of a lesson

Every moment of transition in the school day, every 'start-up', generates inevitable tension and so is a possible source of trouble. Probably the most difficult of these moments is the arrival of a class, and probably the hardest of a secondary school teacher's jobs is the settling down of a class at the start of a new lesson. The stability of the junior school means that the return from play-time or dinner is often a matter of picking up the earlier threads. The home classroom and the class teacher are there session after session. A secondary school teacher will meet a number of different classes in a day.

This series of confrontations is one of the most exhausting aspects of the teacher's day, as it requires the rapid adjustment to a different set of personalities, and also requires each time the nervous energy to 'get things going'. Too many young teachers are in fact defeated in the first five minutes as they wait for the class to come in. Whilst waiting for the latecomers, the teacher engages an individual pupil in conversation or sorts out some books. During this gap the rest of the class are building up a crescendo of chatter; some start moving round the room; one or two start an argument; another idly flicks a few pellets. At this stage the teacher decides that all who are coming have arrived, and tries to quell the noise. Just as his voice is being heard with a 'Will you please be quiet' for the third time, two even later latecomers burst through the door. Finding the right words for them would have been difficult anyway, but now the teacher has a double disadvantage. He is flustered from trying to quell the noise and, secondly, his dealing with the latecomers is in front of a gawping class who have nothing to do but watch the telling off. This unconsciously leads the latecomers to play to the gallery, and the teacher to feel that he is in a contest, with the class as umpires – except they are not neutral. If he is wise, he sends the latecomers straight to their seats (he is in real trouble if they prove to have been taken and a fresh argument bursts) and starts the lesson. But by now he is working in a difficult atmosphere and he himself is tense. Only a supreme effort of will, voice, and personality can move from this situation into a satisfactory lesson.

What I have described is no 'blackboard jungle', nor does it imply an especially difficult class. I have not exaggerated or pictured an unusually bad situation. These minor difficulties happen daily and they leave the young teacher barely able to cope with the subsequent lesson. He ends the day tired, disappointed, and faintly puzzled at 'what went wrong'. You will notice that the difficulty has nothing to do with curriculum planning, pupil grouping, or the preparation of teaching material. It is a matter of class management, and the answer for virtually every subject, every age, and every type of pupil grouping is simple: *have something for every pupil to do when they first enter the room.* Do not expect them to wait for each other or for you. Do not have to *call* them to order: do not let them get out of order in the first place.

Starter activities

I describe in Chapter 7 the importance of the rhythm of the lesson and analyse possible sequences. Here I am concerned only with the routine of the initial phase. There can be some significant activity on which each pupil can make an immediate start as soon as he or she comes into the room and without waiting for anyone else. The simplest, where it fits, is for the pupil to be told: 'Spend five minutes looking over last night's homework.' If possible, make the task more specific by focusing the task of checking one or two elements, for example:

'Check the calculation.'
'Make sure you have a good final paragraph.'
'Look especially at the verbs.'

or whatever may be appropriate. A further routine task is to look over a specified paragraph or page in the textbook, in which case the precise reference and the particular object for the task (for example, 'And find the reasons for . . .') should again be on the board in the expected section. Even simpler still, the pupils may be continuing with whatever piece of work they have been working on recently. The aim is to have something they can all do. *Have the full instruction written on the board (in the same place each time) before the pupils arrive.* Tell them as they reach the door individually or in groups.

On other occasions, however, the teacher will have devised a simple short 'limbering up' exercise. If you are in your early months of teaching or if the class is particularly difficult, go to the trouble of setting the slips of paper and/or worksheets out on each desk before the pupils arrive. Once again, your word at the door is reinforced by your written instructions on the board with the details on the paper.

I recommend that this work is normally carried out in complete silence and that you are strict about this. Use the five minutes of silent work to sort out quietly any latecomers, those who have not brought the necessary pen or books, and so on. Then, if the lesson is to involve exposition or question and answer, after the preliminary piece of work, call the pupils' attention and start your talk from the purposeful calm of that activity, whenever possible building on it and growing out of it.

Often, of course, the initial activity will be to 'continue with last week's work'. In this case, the key is to get each pupil into it as soon as he or she enters. Again, do not wait until general talk has started. And you will need to make sure that necessary equipment and books are out in advance.

Oversight

I have stressed throughout that as most misbehaviour is spontaneous rather than long planned, it can be prevented merely by the 'withitness' of the teacher. There is no doubt that the major behavioural problems are what I call 'the constant corrosion of petty indiscipline'. For instance, one survey of secondary teachers showed that 50% declared 'talking out of turn' as the most 'troublesome' behaviour.[15] 'Hindering other children' is a 'troublesome behaviour' cited by 17% of secondary teachers. Whilst not a huge figure, it is very important. Dramatic problems like 'physical aggression' are very rare – less than 1% in that study. Indeed, minor interruptions are the most substantial classroom management problem for the teacher. Much of this book is designed to help the teacher avoid that before it starts.

Young teachers frequently concern themselves with what they should do when there is bad behaviour, not fully realizing that most examples of bad behaviour would not happen if the pupils were under observation and knew it. Thus an important part of classroom technique is maintaining a constant surveillance of everything that is happening in the room. This means that the teacher's position in the room needs thought, as does the posture in which he helps a pupil. For instance, it is almost impossible to keep an eye on the room whilst bending down from a standing position to help a seated pupil, but easy to keep an eye on the room whilst sitting at a desk with a pupil by your side. Obviously it is impossible to see the room if a knot of pupils is between you and the others, or if you turn your back on the class. I have often been told quite clearly by pupils later found misbehaving that the action started when 'Sir was writing on the board with his back to us'.

A particular skill which needs practice is the ability to 'overlap' activities, so that the teacher can keep two activities going at once. Thus you must be able to deal with one pupil's minor misbehaviour, or a latecomer's intrusion into the room, without breaking off completely from the ongoing activity, or without losing the oversight of the room. This involves, for instance, putting in the occasional sweep of the eyes round the whole room whilst talking to one pupil, or changing stance, so that you can see a different section of the room. A classroom method that makes oversight impossible is simply an unsuitable method for school teaching. It is very rare for a pupil, for instance, to throw a piece of paper out of an open window when Miss is looking, but just the kind of thing that can happen when the teacher is deeply engrossed in helping another pupil.

The end of the lesson

The end of a lesson is not merely the end of that lesson; it is part of the sequence that will lead to other lessons or activities in the school and will be remembered at the back of the pupils' minds as a cue for the tone of your next lesson. It should therefore be an orderly and pleasing occasion.

Consider, for instance, a teacher who had 30 Year Eight pupils working fairly well, if a little noisily. The lesson-change signal went precisely on time by the classroom clock. A moment *afterwards* he said: 'Will you be packing up now. The bell's gone.' He *then* tried to gather up some books! Such an end was unfair on the pupils, and did not help the teacher. It was the end of the week; these pupils needed a summing up, a pat on the back, and reassurance that he was pleased with the week and had a plan for the next. What is more, he ought to have got them out dead on time so that they could get to their next teacher on time. The routine should have been something like this:

2.21 (and I mean as precisely as that) (*standing at the front of the room where they can all see, and stopping their work.*): Stop writing now. (*Insist on complete silence.*) I'm sorry to interrupt you when you're doing so well, but my next customers will be here soon. (*Or whatever joke you can manage.*) This week we've all written up our pieces for the exhibition, and I'm looking forward to reading them. Next week we're going to do a longer piece of writing. Collect up your pieces now.

2.22 Without talking, check your name is on each and hand your piece to Omar or David. Will you collect them up please. (*These pupils do, in the usual order.*)

2.23 Please put your books away in silence. Check there are no bits of paper on the floor. (*Omar and David bring the work to you.*)

2.24 Without scraping your chairs, please stand. (*You go over to the door.*)

2.25 (*Bell goes.*): Well, that was a good week, I look forward to seeing you on Tuesday and I'll tell your tutor how well you've done. This row out first, please. (*You stand in the open door, seeing them out, saying the odd word to individuals, and keeping an eye on the corridor.*)

It is normally wise to ask a class to leave the room a group or a row at a time. This is not always necessary with older pupils, larger rooms, or smaller classes. However, avoid a rush and dismiss a line at a time if you are in doubt. If possible, stand in your earlier position against the door jamb. There you can again supervise room and corridor, and at the same time give each pupil a pleasant parting word or a reminder as appropriate.

Pupils' written work

Some of your pupils in the course of the year will lose much of their work, even when they have done well and are proud of it. It is worth thought and care to try to help them avoid this. Consider the various ways of storing work. A junior-school pupil spends almost all the week in one room and keeps all his books in his own desk. He rarely takes them home, and therefore his only organizational problem is to keep that desk tidy enough for the books to be accessible. The secondary pupil, who moves from teacher to teacher, from library to ICT room, and takes books home for homework, has a more difficult organizational problem. This is especially so when the pupils complete some of their work on a word processor and therefore print on separate sheets. How can the teacher help?

A safe approach is to reduce the amount of written work, whether notes or projects, which the pupil has to keep himself. One effective safeguard is to issue the pupil with a simple loose-leaf folder, which is to be used only for the temporary filing of work in progress. (In the case of very long projects, this must mean only for the section being currently worked on.) All written work is done on punched file paper. The 'current' folder is thus *never* handed in, but each piece or section of work that the teacher wants to take away to read is handed in apart from the folder. *Completed* pieces of work, after teacher and pupil have reviewed them, are filed by the teacher in the pupil's personal 'deposit' file, which the teacher stores. From time to time these are issued for sorting, reviewing, and perhaps indexing sessions, and the folder can also be used for notes of individual teacher/pupil talks, other relevant non-confidential material, and so on. These review sessions can be well related to end of Key Stage assessment. Even the scattiest pupil begins to be impressed by the growing body of his work, and the most he can lose at any time is a single piece!

There are of course other patterns. The pupil can use his loose-leaf folder as his cumulative file, handing in only individual pieces as before. He again has only one, but always one, folder to remember. This is less trouble for the teacher, but risks a year's work being lost in one moment. Many schools prefer to use exercise books, which are definitely more economical on paper as work can start immediately after the preceding piece of writing. If you use exercise books, have a clear routine for them. There is little more infuriating than the constant arguments about whether 'Miss' has the book or not, and if it has been lost, who lost it. The old convention of one book for 'classwork' and one for 'homework' is a possible method, but it does not encourage continuity of assignment, and does not fit ICT printing. Better to have an 'A' and a 'B' book or folder, specify which is to be used, make a note in your register, and always have one in and one out. Different courses and tutorial work have different demands, of course, and each teacher will wish to develop her or his own personal routine. It is difficult to change mid-year and worth establishing at the start, telling the appropriate tutors, and preferably sending a note to parents also. They like to know how your system works.

Collecting in and giving out work

A potential trouble point, which disturbs the atmosphere and tempts pupils into misbehaviour, is the returning of work studied by the teacher to the class. In some kinds of learning sequences, such as extended project work, the teacher is not faced with the simultaneous return of 30 pieces of paper, folders, or exercise books. However, frequently, in all kinds of subjects and all kinds of pupil groupings, you have to give out 30 pieces of paper, folders, or exercise books as rapidly as possible.

There is a nostalgic British memory of a schoolmaster of old talking to 30 boys whilst, with calculated inaccuracy, he flings books thorough the air into different directions. No one makes any noise. Every boy is attentive. The teacher's virtuoso display of eccentric marksmanship is rapid, quells the class, and even allows a few teaching points to be made midstream. Those days have long gone! I have seen many lessons founder as the ill-prepared teacher copes with this apparently simple chore.

The teacher revolves hopelessly, trying to give or throw books in criss-crossing directions, not sure which book will come next, or where each pupil is. Those waiting have nothing to do. Those who have received their books give them a momentary glance and join in the fun. Then there are exchanges as some pupils say they have not had their books. The teacher is uncertain who has not had a book, and if not, why not. The whole procedure is protracted by useless disputes.

I suggest a clear and regularly repeated routine. I shall describe it as if, as I have recommended, the pupils are seated in alphabetical order parallel with your class register. However, the basic procedures can stand with only a little obvious modification if the seating does not follow this pattern. The aims of the routine are two-fold: firstly, a clear and well-known routine stops arguments about who has and who has not handed in work; these are not merely unprofitable but sour relationships and tempt any would-be malingerers into exploiting the confusion to cover up their defaulting. Secondly, a clear-cut routine avoids the waiting and confusion in the room.

Collecting in work

When you collect in the books or sheets, do so in a fixed and precisely repeated routine. Preferably follow the seating plan so that the books are in the order of your mark register. Have the books or sheets collected in whilst the pupils are engaged in some sensible activity – never make collecting in an unaccompanied activity during which pupils are expected to wait patiently. They won't. Whenever possible, collect them at a suitable point *during* the lesson – not in the last minutes. This allows the collecting to be done calmly and carefully. It also allows time for you to check up with any individuals who have not handed work in. If you do not wish to go round yourself collecting the work, arrange for *regular* pupils to do it. More than one, to save time; but not too many, to save movement. I like the first and last in the alphabetical sequence to work from either end. Double-check the books or sheets – that is, enter a mark in your register (see p. 53) to indicate that you have received the work from a pupil, and count the pile of work and check that the number tallies with the number of heads in the room.

Quite a proportion of pupils work on the principle that a confrontation postponed may be a confrontation avoided. They therefore do not declare a failure to produce work at this stage, and hope that it will be discovered too late. They will even hand in a book despite the fact that it has no work in it. Too frequently the teacher is sufficiently confused for it to be possible for such a sharp trickster to get away with it and thus to be encouraged to try again. Some teachers therefore prefer the work to be left open on the pupil's desk before collection, and they collect it themselves.

Returning work

The returning of work is naturally the reverse process. Any mark or grade will have been entered into the mark register in advance. The pile is still in seating order. The class are told that the work will be given out shortly, and if there is anything specific that they should look for or do on receiving their book or sheet. At a time when they are engaged on some work, the books or sheets are brought round. This is a simple and unfussy job as the pile is in seating order and a slow walk round the room suffices. You may prefer to do this yourself on most occasions as you can add a quiet personal word to a number of pupils. Separate any teaching comments you might wish to make to the whole class from the actual distribution of the work. This is partly because no one listens if his neighbour has just had a book back, and partly because it is very difficult to teach and hand back simultaneously. There is nothing more baffling than trying to listen to a teacher who is darting around the room with books. A variation on this method is to lay the books out on the appropriate desks before the pupils reach the room. This leads naturally to starting the lesson with the pupils picking up some point from their returned books. One teacher of Science had the excellent scheme of having the books in a manilla folder for each workbench, which was labelled with a colour, and this colour was the same as that for the relevant folder.

Whatever your teaching style you will have to cope with this basic task of collecting and returning written work every week. It is therefore worth working out a routine which:

allows reliable record-keeping;
eliminates disputes;

is quiet and quick;
is simple and efficient;
never keeps the pupils waiting.

Materials, equipment, and textbooks

Many lessons require the frequent use of various kinds of equipment which have to be issued for the particular lesson, one item to each pupil or group of pupils. The handling of these can be a nightmare for a young teacher, and any losses can cause inconvenience, loss of time, and irritation for subsequent lessons.

Distributing

As in every other matter, the starting point is preparation: check in advance that you have sufficient protractors, scissors, test tubes, slides, OHPs, or work-cards, that you know precisely how many there are, and that the supply is ready to hand. Ideally, the equipment is best stored in a sectional tray of some sort that shows at a glance how many items are there and if any are missing. Preferably, small items, such as scissors, should be stored in trays or racks that hold sufficient only for one-third or half of the class. This speeds up distribution and collection. An obvious example of such storage is pencils: kept and displayed in a block of wood with drilled holes, their checking is easy. Chime bars for Music lessons are a different example of the same need. A compartmental shallow drawer for, say, eight, with a beater in each compartment, makes it possible to see at a glance that each chime bar and beater has been returned. Or you may prefer to store the beaters separately in racks similar to those for test tubes, so that you can see the precise number of beaters at the start and at the finish.

The same principle also applies to the distribution of books or returnable work-cards. If they are pre-piled in, say, tens, there is a clear visual check. Work-cards can be conveniently stored in stout envelopes which have been cut back at the top to reveal the front of the contents.

Whenever you are going to issue anything to the whole class, announce what is going to be issued and how: for example, 'The girl at the front of each row will bring the tray down the row. Take one each.' Add clearly the number that there are to start with, and when they will be collected; for example, 'There are ten in each tray; that's 30 altogether. I shall collect all 30 into the trays a quarter of an hour before the end of the lesson.' It is then a good idea to write the number of items on the board in a prominent position (a regular position if yours is an equipment-orientated subject such as Music or Science):

Tuesday, 11 November
30 rulers

Collecting

If you have taken care over the preparation and issuing, collection and checking will be easy. Do not leave it to the last minute, but do make sure the pupils have something else to do whilst the collection is going on. Nothing is more boring than collection as a sole activity. Give due warning: 'We'll collect the rulers in five minutes.' Then announce the collection method clearly, preferably using the same pupils as those who did the distribution: 'Will the girls in the front of each row please take a tray each and collect a ruler back from everyone in that row. We started with 30 rulers, and I shall check that we have 30 back.' The front girls then do the collection whilst the pupils are doing some writing. Rapidly check the returned trays to make sure each is complete. If one tray has an item short, confidently go down that row at once, saying: 'There's one more to come from this row still.' When you have completed the checking, which should be very quick, let the class know that all is well: 'Good, we have every one of the 30 rulers back.' It is worth declaring this, both because you want the message to be taken clearly that you always check and always know, and also because it ends the lesson with a certain feeling of satisfaction. Pupils *like* being members of a well-run and well-behaved group.

If you have not received all the items back, make an immediate and confident fuss. It is a difficult question of tact to decide how much fuss. You will see why initial checking is so important: you cannot in all conscience challenge a class to 'Return the missing lens' if you are not absolutely sure how many you started with. You will also see the value of the sectional storage and distribution: it narrows the missing item down to one sector of the class. In specialisms with technician support, it is wise to plan the issue and collection of equipment with the technician when possible. If you are indeed confident that a lens, a magnet, a pair of scissors, a book, or a chime-bar beater is missing, my advice is to hold the class and send immediately for a senior colleague. If you do this on the first occasion when an item is missing, the problem will not recur. Teachers in Science, Music, Maths, Arts, and D&T especially, have to be willing to be very firm and to call for support to find the missing item *immediately*. To allow a group to get away with a stolen ruler is to collude with the theft. To regard some items as too small to worry about is to encourage larger thefts.

Textbooks

The use of textbooks and the teaching of how to get the best from them is a core teacherly art. The issuing of textbooks has to be recorded. No school can afford to replace losses, and pupils are more careful with books that they know have been recorded. If there is more than one copy of a title, there is always the possibility of confusion about which copy has been returned by whom. Thus copies in a set of the same title require a serial number clearly stamped in a known place inside the book – as well as a clear indication of the school's ownership and a proper label for the current borrower's name. Enter the serial number in the class register for safe return of the book.

There is no doubt that the kind of procedures which I have described are economical of time in the long run, and apply equally to mixed-ability or setted work, to 'formal' or 'informal' methods, to 'discovery' or 'didactic' lessons. You must get the apparatus and the books out quickly and you must get it all back efficiently.

The use of textbooks

At a time when teachers are ensuring that they make good use of ICT, it may seem strange to emphasize the importance of skilled use of and teaching about the textbook. However, it is clear from research studies in the late 1990s and after, that enabling pupils to make good use of a textbook is a skill that many teachers find difficult. Only one teacher went as far as to report: 'Wider reading is not usually encouraged . . . unless as a punishment'! But many teachers did not give sufficient consideration to developing pupils' needs as readers for learning in that subject. The textbook is not only to help the teacher with facts and illustrations, but to encourage the pupil to explore, reconsider, practise finding out, and extending the teacher's introductory exposition. The research found that the teachers in the sample were 'not apparently giving much practice in reading', and were not advising on 'higher-level reading skills: using an index, skimming, consulting a glossary, selecting relevant text, interpreting illustrations'.[16]

Sadly many schools do not have enough resources, especially for Key Stage Three, for a book for each pupil so that they can take it home for homework. This is especially important, for instance, in Science, History, or Geography when the homework involves re-studying an explanation – not merely using the book (as often in Maths) only for the questions in an exercise. This advice is obviously relevant only if you are able to issue a book to each member (or perhaps 'one between two') of a class. For a young class explain how to make use of such a book:

i   Introduce the book, and what it is for.
ii Tell them all to look at the title page and the contents list. Relate the contents headings to the overall aim of the book.
iii Draw the class's attention to the sub-headings in chapters, their use, and the fact that sometimes you only read certain sections.
iv If there is a glossary, have them turn to it, explain what the title means, and the helpfulness of using it.
v   Have them turn to the index and ensure they know what it is for and how to use it (for example, the sub-alphabetical order for sub-sections).
vi Take a key page and use it to help them see such points as how the text relates to illustrations.
vii Use a paragraph as an exercise in the patterns of prose being used.

As the sequence of lessons develops, sometimes give specific instructions to 're-read pages x to y', or 'look ahead to the conclusion of Chapter 3'. A few pupils take very easily to textbooks. However, most of their reading so far has been of narrative fiction, which uses different overall structure and the paragraphs and sentence structures of which differ very much from non-narrative exposition in textbooks. This makes most pupils inexperienced readers of such books, and they require specific contextual teaching in their textbook-using courses.

Ofsted inspectors have noted in their school inspection reports some examples of the integrated *use* of course textbooks:

> 'The teacher cleverly brought together information from the class textbook and visual material to enable pupils to study medieval farming.'
>
> 'Staff development initiatives have helped teachers to gain a good understanding of issues relating to literacy.'
>
> 'Lessons are usually planned around textbooks.'
>
> 'Students are helped to learn how to use textbooks through regular reference to them in lessons.'
>
> 'Textbooks are used well by teachers.'

Worksheets, and so on

In the previous section I have concentrated on the issuing of equipment, apparatus, and textbooks. To some extent worksheets involve the same procedures. But in addition, there is for them the problem of explanation and of the pupil's need to read. These problems have nothing to do with security and apply equally to disposable sheets which you will not be collecting up. When issuing a worksheet, map, or diagram, remember that for most pupils it is difficult to listen carefully *and* scan a fresh page. Therefore divide the process into three:

● Explain that a sheet is about to be given to each pupil. It is about such-and-such; its purpose is so-and-so; and each pupil will be expected to do this or that. 'When you first get the sheets, put your name in the box . . .' (It is vital that each pupil has a clear task to do when the sheet is received.)

- Have the sheets given out as rapidly as possible, and in silence – yours and theirs! (It is futile to call out instructions *over* a distribution process.)
- After a moment for the task, call for attention. Explain the purpose of the sheet briefly a second time. Take the pupils through its sections. Give the instructions for action a second time. Ask for questions. Only then can the pupils start work on their own. Without this careful procedure there will be a scatter of questions, the answers to which will not be heard by the whole class as most will still be reading.

There will be many occasions when pupils are expected to draw a fresh assignment sheet or a set of teacher-prepared sheets, at their own timing according to their completion of their last task. In such cases, the various sheets or cards are likely to be part of a consistent series, and it is then worth a patient initial lesson making quite sure that the procedures and conventions of the cards are thoroughly understood.

Supplies

Many lessons are going to require pupils to have access throughout to fresh supplies, especially of paper, sometimes of assignment sheets, books, or chemicals. Establish a clear and unvarying prominent position for the supply. If a great deal of paper is used, two piles on either side of the room, under your eye, should be put out regularly before each lesson. If you have ICT work-positions to which pupils move on occasions, have a clear procedure. It is often worth fixing a route to avoid chair scraping and pushing. Make it clear whether permission has to be sought, or if the pupil in need may merely leave his chair to fetch the material. If in the early days you make position, manner, and mode clear ('No dashing!'), in the future this servicing of the learning will normally go smoothly. Never have to delve into a stockroom mid-lesson. An almost invariable rule is to do without that which you have not brought.

Moving furniture or regrouping

One of the most rapid ways to produce chaos is to instruct a group as a whole to move themselves, or even worse themselves and some furniture, to a new, vaguely described position. 'Get your chairs round me' or some such general instruction is a formula for noisy, lengthy muddle, with lost tempers and bruised shins. Yet it is fairly often necessary to arrange such regroupings. Pupils may need to be reseated in a closer group to watch a presentation; they may need to break into small discussion groups; for a competition, they may need to face inwards in two teams; two classes may need to come together in one room to watch a video; in a drama class, a special seating arrangement may be necessary for some group activity; in Circle Time in a Tutorial session a major rearrangement is required. In all cases, it is the teacher's job to *organize* such a move to make it as economical of time, effort, and temper as possible. Such a move will not be achieved successfully without careful and precise teacher direction, unless it is a frequent manoeuvre which works to a regular routine.

The art of directing a large group of pupils in any complicated manoeuvre is to break the group down so that reasonably small numbers carry out clearly understood actions in turn. This means that the teacher must first be clear exactly what is required. I have seen a whole class moving with chairs above their heads, knocking into each other and jockeying for position in the new arrangement, with the teacher trying to shout over the top some new set of directions. Be clear where you want the pupils, and be sure they will fit in the new positions.

Then call for complete silence and attention. Explain that you are about to give some directions for movement, but that *no one is to move until they are actually told to do so*. This last is a vital convention to establish and needs building habitually into every set of movement instructions. Otherwise, with the very best of intentions, pupils start moving and following the teacher's instructions in mid-sentence. Others then follow them; the teacher stops the instruction to tell them to wait; the first lot move back and knock into the next wave. Minor chaos again reigns. Therefore get used to warning 'No movement until I say so' *before* you start delivering the instructions.

Then state specifically which pupils, in which order, are to move to which position. Normally it is best to give the instructions in sections, having each sub-group of pupils move at the appropriate moment. Thus the problem may be to regroup the pupils *and their chairs* in a tight semicircle of two rows in a part of the room where there is space so that, shall we say, they can provide a concentrated audience for three pupils who have prepared a small dramatic reading or performance. The best way to do this would be to tell the pupils earlier that, before they have finished their writing, you will be telling them how to move to their special seating. At the appropriate moment tell the three performers to stay in their seats. Say: 'The row by the door *only*, when I say so, lift your chairs quietly, walk down the aisle and, in the same order, put your chairs down facing the performers' table. Right, *move*, please.' After that group has settled, a similar instruction brings the middle row. Then the first half of the window row joins the semicircle. And finally the last five in the middle row move to sit on the window benches. In this way you reseat the class quickly and quietly, by dividing the larger group into sections and giving instructions and initiating movement for only one section at a time.

Modern teaching frequently uses group work. There are therefore going to be times when the teacher requires the class to change into group positions. A good practice is to note the groupings in the register by a designated letter against each pupil's name. Then call out the names of 'Group A', and ask them to move. And then 'Group B'. Thus you avoid criss-crossing movements and traffic jams with the legs of upraised chairs clashing and locking.

Moving rooms

There is a similar problem if the class is to be taken mid-lesson from their normal room to another classroom, for instance to use the ICT specialist room, to the library, or for a fire drill. If the teacher goes first, she cannot lock the door behind her and she cannot be sure that two or three do not linger. If she follows last, she cannot be sure what is happening at the front, nor what will happen when the first reach the new venue. Either way, the line will straggle. There is a necessary two-stage procedure which works: the teacher goes to the door as for normal dismissal from the room. Before instructing the class to lead on, she tells them to line up in the corridor just outside her room. She then supervises the exit, locks the door, goes to the *front* of the line, and only then starts the second stage of leading the pupils on. This two-stage procedure makes the whole exercise much easier and more pleasant.

The general rule is simple: do not involve your pupils in movement unless it is really valuable. If you really want the movement, give precise instructions for sub-groups of pupils only at one time. To be able to move a full class of pupils is a necessary skill for a teacher.

Curtains, blinds, and screens

One wishes one could do without them, but most of us teach in rooms with the three hazards of cords, blinds (or curtains), and screens. Indeed, teachers without blackout or screens frequently ask for them to be fitted. But they can be the source of a great deal of trouble – as can ordinary windows. Closing the curtains, raising a blind, or lowering a roller screen are all tricky operations. If the operator pulls too hard or lets go too quickly, the resultant danger can not only be a nuisance but will probably leave the offending object in such a way that another person will seize it later and damage it still further.

At the start of the lesson, as the Year Nine come noisily in, the first bunch sees a television monitor.

'Is it a video today, sir?' one asks.

The teacher should have set the equipment up in advance, but he is still untangling the leads, and is slightly nervous about inserting the video cassette. 'Yes,' he shouts, 'and settle down quickly.' This, of course, is never likely to happen after such a vaguely phrased exhortation delivered in the direction of the back wall as he hurries to the mains socket.

'Do you want the curtains shut?' a helpful girl yells out.
'Of course, dope!' a girl calls back. 'Do you think we're going to see a video in this sunshine?'
'I'll do them,' a boy offers.

The teacher is too busy with the recalcitrant video slot to do more than yell, 'Yes, but be careful.'

His wishful thinking is disappointed as two boys go for one curtain. Another unravels a blind cord, and it comes down with a heavy thump, which tells the informed ear that it will never rise again. Another curtain has apparently stuck, and a yank in the reverse direction from a boy, who (as pupils usually do) is hanging on as low down the curtain as possible, tears the rufflette tape off for two feet or so.

After the video, a blind hangs forlornly, one curtain will not return, another has a gash where it caught the corner of an open window, and a third limps from the torn rufflette. These, of course, then require extra care, but actually get even rougher, despairing treatment. And all this from well-meaning, well-motivated, helpful pupils.

The safest way is to determine in advance that only you will touch whichever of these hazards your room boasts. Announce this clearly and stick to it. If you feel this is too restrictive a way, and you will need the curtains closed too often for this, insist that only those pupils whom you instruct are ever to touch these items. You can then give specific instructions to certain pupils to carry out certain tasks. You can appoint one girl to a screen and one to each pair of curtains. They can have a little tuition in the quirks and delicacies of each. They will think 'Sir is a bit fussy', but they will be proud of their task and their expertise – and your curtains, blinds, and screen will continue to serve you.

Leaving the room

Well-meaning, sympathetic teachers are often perplexed by the requests they receive from pupils who ask to leave the room for a variety of personal or apparently educational reasons. The curt advice of those who say 'Never believe a word' seems harsh and hardly helpful to an understanding relationship, and yet the suspicion nags at the back of the mind that there *is* an unusually large number of requests and some pupils do seem to be thoughtlessly flitting in and out. Then comes some crisis, perhaps an accusation of vandalism or petty pilfering, and the teacher feels guilty at not having had a tighter regime. There is also a real, though often unconscious, temptation for teachers having control difficulties to allow a very high number of pupils out of the room to go to the library, the lavatory, to pick up forgotten books, or to check up on this, that, or the other. I found some American high schools countering what they dubbed this 'clean-house policy' by issuing each teacher with one wooden tally. Only the tally was accepted as identification by the corridor security patrols, and thus the teacher could let only one pupil out at a time. Such a system is alien to our schools but it is a reminder that the problem is worldwide.

A teacher's classroom responsibility is to help the pupils learn. This normally involves keeping them in the learning room. Any learning reasons for sending a pupil out should be carefully pondered, authorized by the school's system, and identified by a timed and dated note from the teacher. Personal reasons, such as visiting the lavatory or collecting a book, should be reduced to an absolute minimum. It is perfectly possible for almost all pupils on almost all occasions to be ready for a lesson and not to require to go out again. If you make this clear, the need arises less. Remember also, any pupil who is giving you trouble in a class is likely to give trouble to the librarian, and to cause trouble in corridors, on staircases, and in lavatories. Furthermore, her return is likely to be another of those disruptive moments. A few pupils will have a medical note referring to the medical need to use the lavatory. Also a pupil with no such medical problems will sometimes have such an urgent need. The sensitive teacher will respond after careful questioning and sometimes accept the need.

Of course, there are many important curriculum reasons for pupils' leaving their classroom, such as visiting the library, using a specific ICT facility, or checking some data. Indeed, there are occasions when colleagues in different arts or design disciplines move pupils between rooms for curriculum reasons. Most schools have clear staff policies on when pupils could be sent out of the classroom. All these occasions should be documented and the pupil sent out should carry a note.

Getting the teacher's attention

The accepted convention, which pupils take to readily, is for the pupil who needs the teacher's attention to raise his or her hand. If this convention is to work pleasantly and efficiently for teacher and taught, there are three simple and obvious common sense rules:

- The teacher must be able to see the raised hands! This means the teacher being in a position to see.
- The pupils must be discouraged from asking too often or too readily. Do not misunderstand this remark, or interpret it as being callous. A little simple arithmetic shows that however hard you work, too many raised hands means no one gets a satisfactory reply.
- The raised hand should not need a call. If you allow 'Sir, sir, sir!', no one will be able to concentrate.

These simple procedures are a sensible form of courtesy to the pupils as well as helping to keep the teacher's sanity. They are basically those operated in adult committees and meetings, and this is a point worth making to the class. They also serve the needs of gender equity: classroom observation has shown the tendency of more boys than girls to demand the teacher's attention by strenuous calling.

The question of noise

One of the greatest problems is the almost theological one of defining 'reasonable noise'. Frequently, a teacher feels that some talking is not only reasonable but desirable, but finds the level rises until he or she cannot be heard and very few people can work. I suggest that pure silence is often easier, fairer, and more pleasant. It also releases the teacher to help individuals instead of acting as a continuous noise queller. The teacher must therefore decide when talking is really useful to the activity, as for instance in group experiments in Science. Criteria for what talking is acceptable and what is not should be defined in advance. Too often one hears vague, broadside criticisms thrown at a class in an attempt to control what has become by even the most accepting standards unacceptable noise:

'That's quite enough noise, 2L.'
'You're getting too noisy again, you know.'

These remarks, which have to be shouted above the ongoing noise and thus add to it, are too vague to give any pupil a clear instruction. Indeed, rhetorical questions are as a rule inadvisable and cause some confusion. Perhaps the worst I have heard was the desperate shout: 'Will you make less noise and do more work!'

These pleas have insufficient clarity. The general hubbub is marginally reduced for a short time, and then it builds up to the same or an even worse level.

If talking is to be allowed, the criteria can usually be defined more precisely and helpfully by legislating about to whom the talking may be directed:

'You may talk to your partner, but *not* across the gangways or to anybody in a different row.'
'Members may talk to anyone within their group, but you must not talk to anyone in another group.'
'Only one person at a time may talk, and the group leader, who is chair, will decide who is to talk next.'

It is more difficult to define acceptable voice levels, as the distinction between 'talking' and 'shouting' is vague, and hardly sensed by many young people. Nevertheless, instead of directing criticisms to the class as a whole about the level of noise as a whole, it is possible to pick patiently on each of the loud pupils one by one (for there is usually a handful who are considerably louder than the others), speak to them individually, and by a mixture of joking and firmness to train them to speak 'quietly'. If you do not, they will be the ones who ignore your general pleas to the whole class, and they will act as pacers, encouraging the whole class gradually to get louder and more disruptive week by week.

There is an easy assumption that for some reason or other talking is a necessary part of all mixed-ability work. Certainly, talking for a purpose is an essential part of much learning. Detailed research has usefully emphasized that for us. However, that does not mean that it is valuable *all* the time. Much individual work, especially reading and writing, requires an atmosphere of concentration. For these activities the silence of a public library is normally far more successful than 'reasonable noise', and is much appreciated by most pupils. Indeed, it is more enjoyable to have clearly defined contrasts between the 'co-operative talking' and the 'library silence' sessions than it is to have all lessons at roughly similar level of interruptive noise, with the teacher struggling to regulate the volume every fifteen minutes or so.

Helping the individual

One of the greatest technical problems, and one which ruins many good intentions, is how to give individual help to pupils. It is a necessary part of much teaching. Yet so often all that happens is that no one gets any real attention and the general class atmosphere makes it difficult for anyone to work. *Effective personal help requires ruthless method.* If you are to have a proper consultation with a single pupil, you must be reasonably sure you will not be interrupted by other pupils. There is little more depressing for a pupil than the kind of lesson where the teacher is starting a few words to one pupil, breaks off to shout across the room, moves to another pupil, starts working with him, and turns in mid-sentence to quell trouble in another corner. I have seen this happen in lesson after lesson.

I remember one well-meaning and intelligent teacher with considerable presence who easily reduced a class to a frustrated muddle. She was constantly and exhaustingly on the move and could never oversee the room. Concentration was made more difficult by 'Miss, miss, miss!' continuously from all over the room. The situation reminded me of a hotel waiter I was told of years ago in a large hotel lounge at teatime. He eventually became so irritated by the finger-snapping and whistles that he flipped up the tails of his tailcoat, declaring: 'I may have a tail, but I am not a dog!'

A teacher, similarly, is not a dog to be called like that. A teacher who finds this happening should ask himself why the pupils call. It is firstly that if one is allowed to, the others feel they must. Secondly, if the teacher constantly roves, he usually has his back to many of the pupils at any one time, thus forcing them to add voices to hands to catch attention. The teacher is exhausted and confused by the constant swivelling around, as he is tugged hither and thither. Indeed, constant patrolling can be counter-productive. It is wise to target your interventions, rather than moving like a cocktail waiter, looking for those who might need something extra. What is very difficult is deciding when to try and keep all the pupils moving at the same pace in the same way, and when to accept, and even encourage, differences of ways of moving forward. What is known as the 'conveyor-belt classroom', when the teacher tries to move everyone along at the same rate – struggling to stop some falling off at the other end, while endeavouring to ensure that slow starters have clambered on – can be limiting. Whilst there should be overall class direction, your class is a gathering of individuals who need individual encouragement.

An effective solution

The number of individual pupils you can specifically teach in a lesson is limited if you are really going to help them. It is therefore better to reduce the number, but give effective help, and to keep a record so that you know clearly who has been seen and who missed. This may mean staying at your desk in the front of the room to do your individual helping. You are comfortable and stable, and able to talk more coherently. You can more easily keep the others quiet by a look without interrupting your work with the pupil. You have your mark-register at hand to enter comments. The pupils know where you are. You can have a chair by your side, and call pupils up with their work and Diary to sit by you for a few minutes at a time.

Obviously, in a practical lesson, such as Science or D&T, the teacher must move to the apparatus. It is then necessary for a very strict agreement that no one calls out. It is usually best to move in a regular circuit of the pairs or groups so that, even though you are on the move, the class have a sense of your direction.

Whatever you do, do not bury yourself in a knot of pupils, thus encouraging the others to cause a disturbance.

ICT workstations

Many classrooms will have a number of ICT keyboards. The management of their use is much harder than if every pupil has her or his own laptop, although even then there is the problem of moving to and using the printers. As with all apparatus, such as in a Science or D&T workroom, there needs to be a clear routine and set of procedures for *this* room, which may be rather different for a number of reasons from another specialism or another room. Of course, many but not all pupils will have a keyboard at home. Often, therefore, they need very clear instruction on the pattern of use in your classroom – where they cannot go to and from the ICT keyboard as they can at home.

Group work

All that I have said applies equally to working in groups and to working as a class or individually. However, group work brings with it advantages and difficulties in management. For instance, the advantage of giving pupils opportunities to co-operate can be lost if either rows or jokes become common. As the teacher is in a less dominant position, it is often hoped that teacher–pupil relationships will be better. Too often, however, there is a bad effect on the teacher–pupil relationship, as the teacher turns into a wandering nagger, constantly harrying groups along, rarely able to teach, and thus losing satisfaction as the pupils lose their contact with him.

Decide whether group work is likely to help in your particular situation by assessing the needs of the class, the curriculum aim, and the advantages of working in groups. Groups offer the need to co-operate. They are therefore a better situation for planning, deducing, or analysing. Furthermore, a small group offers the opportunity for pupils with more precisely defined qualities to interact (for example, friends, withdrawn pupils, verbally able pupils, mechanically minded ones, a mixture of abilities). It is unlikely, even in Science or Drama, that all the work benefits very much from these characteristics, and the first essential of your planning is to *decide when and for what activities work in small groups is really best* (not, usually, for reading or writing).

Your decision about which activity to concentrate on will determine the composition of the group. There is a great deal of confused thinking about the use of small groups, especially about whether the aim is to reproduce the full-class mixture in the smaller group or give the opportunity of specially focused appropriate help to groups with roughly the same needs. Many inexperienced teachers automatically presume that 'group work' means work in self-chosen groups. There are three main grouping strategies:

1 Entirely mixed-ability

This grouping is especially good for the verbal interaction of the less able pupils in activities that do not depend too much on intellect – for example, planning a play in Drama, observing an experiment in Science, devising a sound pattern in Music, or interviewing a visitor in a tutorial session.

2 Chosen for a specific quality

This criterion may be necessary for emotional reasons or intellectual ones. For instance, it is often extremely difficult for shy and withdrawn pupils to join in group work in Drama in a group that has talented extroverts. A specially chosen 'shy' group can work better on occasions. Similarly, in some scientific work pupils who have difficulties with computation may be better working together, so that they can be given special help and will participate. When group work is used in languages, pupils are usually best with others of their own language attainment. This is sometimes true of bilingual pupils. The decision is influenced by the nature of the activity: will pupils gain or have extra difficulties if the small groups have a mixture of a certain kind of ability?

3 Friendship groups

Obviously self-chosen groups will not necessarily be formed according to the first two criteria. For certain activities, old friendships will help by offering security and support. *For others, precisely the opposite effect will result.* The arguments I gave earlier about pupil seating (p. 45) apply even more forcefully here.

Arranging the groups

Having decided when to break into groups and which kind of group, tell the pupils of the plan and the grouping method. If you simply slip into your explanation of the Art project or the Maths scheme '… and we shall work in groups', there will be a tic-tac display of signalling across the room for surreptitious recruiting, which will completely blot out your explanation from the pupils' minds. Make it clear how the groups will be arranged:

> 'I have already divided you up into five groups.'
> 'Your group letter is on the top of the work I handed back.'
> 'You can choose your own groups during break, and write down the names of those you wish to work with before we meet again.'

Often teachers plan groups in their mark-books, sometimes having lettered heterogeneous groups and numbered homogeneous ones, calling on them as appropriate. It is very rarely wise to allow self-chosen friendship groups for I have found in subjects as diverse as Mathematics and Drama that the results are less good.

What size should the groups be? This depends on the characteristics of the activity, the room, and the pupils. For most rooms, six groups is the maximum that can work separately without mutual distraction. Four or five is better in a normal-sized room – one in each corner and one in the centre. Science labs or Art rooms are usually larger and can take more groups. Subjects that work in smaller class sizes can similarly have smaller groups.

As for the size of the group, four or occasionally five seems the ideal number for most activities. If the group is above six, a leader is required and problems of control start up. If the group is below four, interaction can become less profitable. When explaining the scheme, remember to take account of an awkward total number in the class, for example, with, say, 27: 'We'll have six groups of four and one of three.'

Working with the groups

The teacher must brief the class very closely about the task of each group. Usually the tasks should be precisely defined, often involving reporting back. Ensure clear instructions about time limits and how feedback from the groups are given.

Whilst the groups are operating, the teacher's role is difficult. Above all, you must retain overall control. Far from group work being the key to class control, as some teachers optimistically hope, *class control is the key to group work*. For part of the time you may have to stand in your central focal point merely giving out a benign but firm look and nudging one or two pupils into their group activity by a look. Later you may wish to walk around *without intervening* but simply looking encouragingly at each group close to. These two tasks are necessary, for the work of the group is likely still to depend on your observable interest, seen from afar.

The most difficult task is to give more precise encouragement to each group. It is a great skill to be able to visit each group quickly and effectively, and one which is acquired only by conscious practice. Therefore, be clear what enquiry you are going to make to each group, and avoid a cosy little chat. Make your enquiry precise:

'What colours have you seen in the test tubes?'
rather than:
'And how's it all going?'

'What scale have you chosen for the plan?'
rather than:
'And is the plan working out?'

Normally you will have to settle for one or two such enquiries, a comment on the answer, or a phrase of encouragement, and you will move on. Move irregularly but calmly, so that your circuit is not regular enough for skivers to know when you will reach them. If another group does make a distracting noise whilst you are working with one group, finish what you are doing and then move across. If points of general value strike you as you observe the work of various groups, save the points up. You can then stop *all* the work and make one group of points to the whole class from a good focal point. Do not throw out snippets of advice to the whole class unexpectedly from different corners of the room.

When you use group work, be judicious in choosing your opportunity, thoughtful in the composition of the groups, specific in your instructions, and firm in your overall control.

6

The teacher's performance

An enthusiastic person preparing for teaching is likely to have a range of expectations and to consider subject knowledge and relating to young people as the crucial, perhaps the only, real concerns. She may discuss many aspects of a teacher's role, sometimes disparaging the 'social work' aspect. Very few teachers in training and even fewer commentators speak of the role of 'teacher as performer'. Indeed, many would fear that the concept of 'performer' is highly unsuitable – almost false. Is not 'performance' a pretence? How is it possible to take curriculum statutory demands seriously if you 'perform'?

However, my experience and observation convince me that, whether they like it or not, all secondary school teachers are to some extent performers. A teacher of a group of pupils is often projecting herself to the group. She will neither convey the sense of an explanation nor the feeling of her reaction unless she has developed ways of amplifying and projecting. Of course, a very great part of a teacher's task is small-group or individual interaction: asking just the right question to a pupil who has misunderstood a Maths issue or giving the most appropriate words of praise to a pupil who has completed a design in technology is vital and difficult. These skills do not compete with or replace, but complement, the more public skills of whole-group presentation. For a significant part of his or her professional life every teacher is a performer, using voice, facial expression, posture, and gesture.

Every teacher has to cultivate a certain air of confidence. This does not mean being overbearing, or brash, or domineering. There is, though, in any audience (and you forget at your peril that, however you are teaching, the pupils are often an audience) a subtle sixth sense that alerts them to a lack of confidence in the person 'out there'. In pupils, as in music hall audiences of the past, there is further an instinct that drives them to test that hint of a lack of confidence, and to split the person apart if it proves as weak as it appears. This is neither to recommend insincerity nor to demand constant volume. A teacher needs to be true to her- or himself, and 'performing' ability is part of that. To be 'larger than life' is not to be false to life, but it is to select and develop. In this section I shall consider various aspects of this idea of 'performing'.

Appearance

The days, in most secondary schools, have long gone since Headteachers felt able to venture an opinion on teachers' dress, still less to proffer advice. Yet, there is no doubt that clothing speaks: the teacher's clothes and appearance are an important part of classroom success. I have argued continually that the school in general and the classroom in particular are not just 'any old places', and that they have their necessary conventions. A teacher's clothing is part of that, and the pupils have certain expectations.

The first of these is an only half-conscious feeling that 'if he cares about us, he'll care about how he looks for us'. It is a normal expectation that respect and care for a situation will be reflected in care over the individual's appearance, and that this care, whatever its stylistic manifestation, will be revealed in cleanliness, good condition, and obvious signs of considered and personal choice. Most parents, whatever their social position or cultural background, dress carefully and somewhat formally for visits to school. It is an insensitive fallacy to think that these parents are made to feel more at their ease by teachers dressing over-casually.

Similarly, it is an odd and inaccurate interpretation of social class to presume, for instance, that children from deprived inner-city areas prefer their teachers to be either scruffy or avant-garde. Still stronger, most pupils and parents from minority ethnic backgrounds are clearly more at ease with professionals who choose to display the slightly more impersonal and respectful (the other side of 'respectable') clothing of the public conventions of the world. They find it less than confidence-giving that some teachers ostentatiously reject the style of doctors, lawyers, shop managers, and civil servants. That wider convention, labelled 'formal', usually gives parents a greater sense of ease and confidence as they can relate what they see to the wider conventions of the society they know.

Most pupils' preferences are fairly clear: they like their teachers to be individually dressed, interestingly but not too unusually, colourfully but not too strikingly, neatly but not too staidly. They are thrown by the slightly aggressive uncertain choice of whatever is currently the way-out vogue; they are depressed by the badly worn; and they are quietly insulted by the torn or dirty.

Speaking to the class

There are going to be many times when you need to speak to the whole class. These must be a success, both because pupils enjoy being members of a class and these 'whole-class' moments are therefore important to them, and because the content in all its aspects (including feeling and attitude) needs to be entirely clear to all. Furthermore, if you cannot succeed on these occasions, that elusive control of the group will slip away from you. There are three clues to speaking to the whole class:

> choose your moment;
> decide what you are going to say;
> use a suitable manner.

Choose your moment

If everyone needs to hear, you must make sure everyone does. Conversely, if everyone does not need to hear it, do not trouble to say it! A suitable moment must relate both to the function of what is being said and to the mood of the group. For instance, it is a bad moment while a few are not yet in the room or while the class are putting materials away. You can see many teachers suddenly thinking of something that they think the class ought to know. All the pupils are busying around; the teacher suddenly starts throwing out a scatter of advice. No one is ready for it; many do not stop to listen; most others do not hear. Never pepper a buzz of activity with general instructions at odd moments. Such ill-judged outbursts do more harm than good. *Before you talk to the class, obtain complete silence.*

Be sure you need to talk. Gather in your mind all that you need to say. ('And one last thing ...' is often used to introduce three or four points!) Then position yourself sensibly. (Never throw out advice on the move or from a back corner of the room.) Catch attention and silence – completely. A clap or a simple phrase can work.

> 'Right, stop work and listen, please.'
> 'Everyone quiet now!'
> 'Eight B!'

Never start until you have both complete silence and all eyes on you. Remember, you have disciplined yourself not to speak unless it is necessary, and you have not got immediate silence and attention: keep calm and good humoured. Hold your position and pause a moment. In a quieter and friendly tone speak to two or three pupils *by name* :

> 'Mohammed, you've got to put that down now.'
> 'Wendy, look at me.'
> 'Chris, stop talking now.'

(The importance of knowing the individual names is obvious.) A final gathering exhortation is probably necessary now:

> 'Good. Everyone listen carefully!' or
> 'Right, everyone's looking at me, then!'

In some especially noisy situations, such as improvised Drama, PE, or 'workshop' Music sessions, it is often best to use a manufactured sound to call the class to silence. For instance, I have seen a tabor successfully used in Drama, a ball in PE, and a cymbal in Music.

What are you going to say?

The older preacher's rule applies to almost all classroom speech:

> Tell them what you are going to tell them.
> Tell them.
> Tell them what you have told them.

This is not boring: it makes for clarity and, most significantly, gives *confidence* to the listener, who can know where the speaker is going and know that he has grasped what he is meant to grasp. It is always easier to understand the detail of what is being said if the larger direction is clear and can be grasped.

Be concrete and particular. This may mean working up to a generalization by way of specific instances. It may mean making a sandwich of generalization illustrated by examples, and then returning to the generalization.

Use references and comparisons that the pupils are sure to have seen for themselves (or on television) and have already recognized. It is amazing how often we use totally unknown comparisons, for example, rural imagery to urban children.

Get into the way of putting sentences so that the central ideas come out clearly. This means that the key facts should not be subordinated, nor should they linger to the end of a sentence. Grammatically simple sentences are usually better than more sophisticated compound ones. 'Even though ...', 'It was because ...', 'Until they had completed ...', 'The fact that ...' are all examples of cliff-hanger openings that push the main point to the end of the sentence and frequently confuse young pupils. Avoid, then, long compound sentences with strings of parentheses and subordinate clauses. Such a sentence depends on the listener holding sections in his mind until the speaker returns to the main structure. Many pupils will have lost the thread by then.

There is also the problem of vocabulary (or, for pupils, 'Vocabulary is also a problem'). On the whole, this is less serious than syntax, but nevertheless care is needed. Any key technical words should, whenever possible, be written on the board in advance. Then they can be pointed to as you use them, and the sight reinforces the sound. Usually, you will want to avoid the less common words. Notice I do not say 'long' or even 'difficult'. The real test is which words have become familiar from the television and popular papers. Rather than avoid every uncommon or difficult word, slip in an alternative or brief explanation without holding up the flow of the sentence. Indeed, do not avoid the single correct and unambiguous term by well-meaningly but confusingly using a word from the 'polysemous vernacular'. For instance, 'architrave' is easier to explain, understand, and remember than 'the thing that goes round a door'.

Whilst experiencing a word in its context should not often be used for a full etymological analysis, a pause to explain not only the meaning of the word but *how* it has that meaning often helps the pupils really grasp the word. This, by the way, is also a way of including the National Curriculum *Handbook*'s requirement of 'language across the curriculum' positively to support your subject and the pupils' wider understanding of language, including the words of EAL pupils:

> 'Pupils should be taught the technical and specialist vocabulary of subjects and how to use and spell the words.'4

Language for Learning in Key Stage Three properly includes the aim that pupils should 'recognize links between words related by word families and roots'. This has been one of our major weaknesses, with words being defined in different school subjects without the stems and affixes being explained or the connection pointed out with words from other subjects – or even everyday life! For instance, a Key Stage Two Maths textbook declares 'Polygons have straight sides', but does not define 'poly-'. There are over 80 words with 'poly-' as a prefix. Some are little used, but the pupils will meet 'polyhedron' and 'polynomial' later in Maths, and 'polysyllabic', 'polygamous', and 'polymath', for instance, as they widen their knowledge of life. Or take 'syn-' and 'sym-', which have the same meaning and are very common indeed. Pupils should be helped to see the meaning of 'together' in, for example, 'synonym', 'sympathy', 'symphony', and 'symmetry'.

Thus a Science teacher in introducing 'photosynthesis' would pop into the scientific explanation that:

> '"Photo-", as in "photograph", means light, and "syn-", as in "synonym" means "together" – bring light together with the chemicals in the growing plant.'

Incidentally, specialist word charts in large print on the classroom wall, with the stems and affixes pointed up, really help this cross-subject approach to language.

Your manner

Talking to a class-size group is an art, and one that needs practising. It is neither the same as lecturing to a hundred nor as chatting to two or three pupils in the playground. It requires a mixture of both techniques. You need to have the right volume, a suitable range of expression, and the right communication of looks and eyes.

Your voice must be clear, and you must have a sense of speaking to the group. This is a skill that can be learnt. It means pitching your voice adequately for someone at the back, and maintaining that volume. Leave decent pauses in between sentences and do not weaken your remarks with fill-phrases such as 'kind of', 'sort of', 'y'know'. Although the volume must be adequate, the key is intensity and clarity rather than volume. Use the pitch and flow of your voice and the phrasing and pauses to highlight the structure of the sentences.

Pitch your voice a trifle higher than the level strictly required for full audibility, but only a trifle higher. Constant shouting is wearing to teacher and taught. On the other hand, a little spare volume, as it were, is necessary to prevent odd snatches being lost to some pupils. (Although you will sometimes wish to use a deliberately low value for effect.)

If you are faced with a specially large meeting, such as when three or more classes are brought together, perhaps as part of a team-teaching exercise, check first that you can be heard at the extreme back corners. Do not do this by a generalized 'Can you hear me at the back?' This starts an embarrassed or raucous barrage. Instead ask one person specifically: 'John' (or 'The boy by the door') please raise your hand if you can hear me properly.'

Modulate pitch, volume, pace, and tone both to suit the sense of what you are saying and for the almost musical effects that good speaking always has.

Your face should, within sensible limits, reflect your voice. Your expression should change, your eyebrows rise, your mouth snap as the sense demands. It is curiously difficult to follow a deadpan face, as the incongruity between sense and look puzzles the hearer. Similarly, you should gesture economically but significantly.

Finally, the sense of speaking to the actual pupils present rather than merely delivering into the atmosphere comes from the way you manage to look at individuals and scan the group. The key is the communication with your eyes. *Feel* the sectors of the room, and underline the structure and sequence of your remarks by directing your phrases to the different sectors. After a while you will come to do this naturally, using the change of direction as a form of rhetorical punctuation, not too abrupt or dramatic, but sufficient to help those in the room feel that they are a group, and that the words are embracing the entire room. Do not follow a regular circuit, like a radar beam remorselessly scanning the horizon. Think, perhaps, of the arrangements of a five on a dice, take each of the five sectors into your glance from time to time in an irregular order. Within each group, look at only one pupil, a different one each time you return to the sector, and cast your remark to her. Feel that you really are communicating personally with that individual: look her in the eyes, and be aware of her expression. Almost never change direction arbitrarily mid-idea, but articulate the progress of the remarks and the shift of argument by the direction of focus, so that the expressions amplify the sense structure. This way you establish an intimacy with the pupils that always assists order and enriches communication.

Questioning

It is taken for granted that teachers will ask questions, but an analysis of the purpose and method has not been often attempted. The paradox is that questions are, or should be, rarely asked for mere finding out if the pupil knows, but more for actually teaching. That is, although some questions will be checking comprehension or testing recall, very often in asking questions the teacher is helping the pupil to focus and clarify, and thus to have thoughts and perceptions that he or she would not have had otherwise.

When to ask a question, when not to, whom to ask it to, what to ask, how to point the question, how to know if a question is not registering – these are difficult skills. The point of the question is to teach rather than to test. The question should therefore be answerable if at all possible. The skill is then the opposite of the questioning skill in a quiz or panel game, where the zest of battle drives towards 'winning'. The successful teacher's question is precisely one that *can* be answered, not one that cannot be. The devising of the answer should be an intellectual gain, with the pupil using her past knowledge to develop new insights.

Each question should be easy and short, building up a kind of programmed-learning approach to deeper or more difficult points. That way no one feels frustrated by facing the unanswerable, and the pupil is often able to see complex points as the culmination of 'obvious' simple points. This is, of course, as important in helping individuals as it is in full-class questioning, and is a key technique in Science and Maths.

Questions should not normally have a huge range of possible answers, except when you are building up a composite answer. These questions, which one hears so often in the classroom, are what I categorize as the 'Guess what I'm thinking' question: only telepathy can lead to the answer which the teacher has decided is 'the right answer'. Questions should be as specific as possible, and should be as pointed to the precise sequence of learning as possible.

Thus: 'What does a fraction mean?' is not as good as: 'What does the figure beneath the line in a fraction tell you?' Unless you are certain that the pupils fully understand all the terms of a question, avoid asking what is in effect two or more questions in one.

Thus: 'What do the pyramids tell us about the Egyptians?' should be broken down into: 'What did the Egyptians use the pyramids for?' 'Why did they spend so much money and skill on that?'

Gap-filling is, on the whole, an unsatisfactory questioning technique; it encourages mere guessing and does not offer the benefit of a real exchange of thought. The typical kind of statement which ends with a sudden gap and a rising tone of voice to indicate the question also offers the very real difficulty that the pupil does not know a question is coming until it has gone! He then has to replay the tape mentally, as it were, to get back to the start of the sentence before he can answer it. No wonder pupils often bleat utter nonsense words in response to such so-called 'questions'.

Defining words and terms

Think twice before asking for the definition of a word. Abstract words are taxingly difficult to define, even by those who have a very good grasp of their meaning. A definition, furthermore, has to have a universal validity, whereas for the purposes of the learning of the moment only the relevant sense is required. Thus the pupils groping for a full definition are often getting further from the problem rather than solving it. Examples of important words of which this is true are 'energy' in Science, 'relationship' in Maths, 'revolution' in History, or 'develop' in Social Studies.

If you are requiring a definition, you must take trouble to get one. Pupils will more often than not give an instance ('It's when …', 'A person who …'). Thus, asked 'What does "impassive" mean?', pupils answer: 'When a person doesn't show his feelings.' So, if definition is not what you are working at, cast the question in a form that allows an example: 'If his face was "impassive" what would it show?' Try asking any pupil in Years Seven, Eight, and Nine: 'What is an autograph?' Most will answer: 'It's when you're famous, and …'. The teacher, of course, will point out that 'auto' means 'self' (as in 'automobile') and 'graph' means 'writing' or 'drawing'.

Responding to the answers

The teacher has an important and sensitive task in responding to the pupil's answers also. A famous theatre producer, Tyrone Guthrie, once described the stage producer's central job as being 'an ideal audience of one'.[17] *The response is a form of teaching.* If you sit amongst the pupils in many lessons, you will be amazed at the number of answers that get no response at all, or merely a killing dead-flat 'yes'. Always give a clear, colourful, tactful response.

Despite your care, 'wrong' answers will frequently be given. Never mind. Use them for what they are – next steps to further thought – and take up the answer as a challenge for you to devise rapidly the next appropriate question. Never, or almost never, ridicule, but turn the answer to good account. It will be a guide to the pupil's misunderstanding. You need to deduce which route the pupil took to the wrong answer, and use that deduction to help him see for himself the better alternative. This has to be done adroitly. Do not labour the point. Explain a confusion. If there has been a misunderstanding, ask the question which clears it:

'If x is 3, what is $x - 2x$?'
'Minus two.'

(Clearly, the pupil answering has taken $x + 2$ away from x.)

'Oh? Is $2x$ two times x, or two plus x?'
'Two times.'
'Then if x is 3, what does $2x$ equal?'
'Six.'
'Yes, because $2x$ is two times x, and two times 3 is six. Therefore ...'

The idea of clues needs care. If you are to prompt, do so by taking the pupil through the normal thought processes that would lead to the correct answer. Never merely give irrelevant verbal clues. Rhyme and irrelevant association are not helpful to thought. For instance, a Science teacher about to introduce the idea of materials as 'conductors' of electricity said: 'I don't mean bus conductors.' If that connection was to be made it should have been to link the 'leading' that is the meaning of 'duc(t)', as in 'educate' and 'viaduct', but as it was the association merely confused by bringing a picture of a bus to mind.

Other techniques

A central teaching technique which is of great pleasure to the pupils and of great value to their learning is a quick-fire sequence of questions ranging around the whole group, bringing all in, prompting thought, and leading to understanding. As a general rule, always put the question before naming the pupil – otherwise no one else will think. Never start 'Does anyone know ...?' Vary the form and pattern of your questions, both to maintain interest and to make it impossible to guess who will be asked next. This can be an enjoyable game. Frequently require all the class to jot down short answers of one word or so on paper, and then ask one and then another to call an answer out. This not only makes it all like a party game, but also makes everyone participate. Sometimes use a show of hands as a way of making the class vote for one or another answer.

Although almost all teaching sequences involve some questioning, do not be tempted to see a solid questioning sequence as 'discussion'. When asked about the 'method' of a lesson, teachers are three times as likely to call a session 'discussion' as a trained observer in the class would: what is thought of as 'discussion' by the teacher at the front does not always feel like that from the middle or back of the class.

Generally discussion is better managed, whether in small groups or whole-class, if there is a fairly closely focused target for the discussion: to agree a chosen design in D&T, to assess an appropriate reaction in a tutorial period, to develop a hypothesis in ICT. In teacher-led whole-class discussion, the teacher's job is to set the frame, define the intended product, and then act as chair. This role switch from exposition to neutral enabler has to be acted out so that the pupils realize they are not being questioned or assessed, but encouraged to join together to explore ideas. The tutorial period is one of the most important occasions for this, but it is also very useful in the full range of subject courses from Maths to Art.

Reading aloud

Most teachers have to read aloud at some point in their lessons. This is more so in the case of English teachers and only slightly less so for other Humanities teachers. Teachers read a great deal. Even teachers of Maths or Science read aloud a surprising amount – far more than they seem to realize. Indeed, the reading of a brief passage of scientific or mathematical writing often highlights a concept very clearly.

Reading aloud is not a difficult skill, but it is one which is so rarely taught or practised in training that many teachers are extremely bad at it. There are few things more depressing than trying to concentrate on a teacher's dreary reading: voice flat, stumbling, odd repetitions, failures of emphasis, speed a constant plod, eyes glued to the page, no gesture or movement, except for the off-putting, irrelevant pacing around. No wonder a pupil once complained: 'When he reads, he makes it, well … just a stream of words, not any sense.'

A sequence of prose has a rhythm and stress pattern that reinforces the grammatical pattern, which in turn is the key to the underlying sense. Especially with non-narrative prose, the art is to use the flow of the voice, the changes in pitch, and pauses to demonstrate the grammatical sense. For instance, this means allowing the elision of those syllables that are elided in speaking. Keep the normal spoken pronunciation of 'a', 'say', 'had', rather than pedantically filling them out. It requires avoiding unintentional breaks mid-phrase, but the emphasizing of breaks that indicate meaning.

Practise on stories, where there is a real stimulus to animate the words on the page, to stress the dialogue, differentiate the speakers, dramatize the pauses, and read feelingly. Try, for instance, two stories by Bill Naughton,[18] manipulating the copy with one hand and holding the attention of the audience with your eyes. Can you realize the full comedy of *Seventeen Oranges*, when the lad Clem is preparing to steal a cheese from the docks and makes a dummy exit first?

> 'What have you got in there?' asked Pongo, who was the bobby on duty.
> 'A cat,' said Clem, 'but don't ask me to open it, or the blighter will get away.'
> 'A cat?' said Pongo. 'Don't come it. Let's have it opened.'
> Clem wouldn't at first, but when Pongo insisted he got mad, and he flung it open, and out leapt a ship's cat, which darted back along the docks with Clem after it, shouting.

The pause of expectation after 'he flung it open' is a fair test. A subtler example, based on the simple stressing of a word usually unstressed ('did') comes at the ending to a later story in the volume, one which moves the most 'difficult' and recalcitrant classes, *Spit Nolan*:

> Then I heard the ambulance men asking me Spit's name. Then he touched me on the elbow with his pencil and said:
> 'Where *did* he live?'
> I knew then. The word 'did' struck right into me. But for a minute I couldn't answer. I had to think hard, for the way he

said it made it suddenly seem as though Spit Nolan had
been dead and gone for ages.

In all first-person writing, it is especially important to bring out the
speaking voice that lies behind the print. This means capturing the
rhythmic pattern and the natural flow. Non-narrative writing,
especially exposition and argument, is more difficult. Move on to
practise illustrative material from history, and descriptions in
scientific writing. Try and practise articulating the explanations and
questions in a Maths textbook.

The essence of the art of reading aloud is the way the voice
expresses the writer's sense, but the reader's body positions,
occasional gesture, and especially the use of the eyes are also
important. An audience (and when they are expected to listen to a
reading in a classroom pupils are an audience) looking at a reader
whose face is locked onto the book and whose eyes are only
scanning the text gets easily bored. Some teachers, anxious to look
up, then lose their place in the text when they look down again.
There is a simple technique of using one hand to cradle the text and
a finger of the other ready to 'keep the place' as you look up and act
as a safe point of return. It is worth practising reading like this,
standing in front of an imaginary class, and using your eyes to
reinforce the delivery of key phrases to the audience.

In many lessons and tutorial sessions in which pupils develop
their ideas and show their understanding through writing, a
teacher will want to read a selection of good, interesting extracts
from the work of various pupils. The activity, provided that it
does not follow every written assignment as regularly as
clockwork, is an excellent one. It hides, however, a trap for the
unwary: how long will it take you to find the extracts? Will you
find them in the best order to make your points? What will the
pupils do whilst they are waiting between extracts? If you are to
use this vivid didactic device, prepare it: choose and mark your
passages in advance. (Self-adhesive, transparent stickers with
coloured tabs are extremely practical technology for this.) Arrange
them in the order you want, and even rehearse a slick
performance.

Instructions

A significant element of a pupil's day is receiving instructions. Some of these are routine and others unexpected and even complicated. The teacher wishes that all of them would be accepted gracefully, understood, and carried out. It seems simple to tell someone what to do, but in fact it is a tricky craft, and some teachers regularly produce confusion rather than the expected action.

However, there are simple techniques to giving groups instructions, which can be analysed, practised, and polished. The starting point is as for talking to the class: they must *all* be silent and still: 'Everyone please stop talking, keep quite still – stop reading, writing!' Only then give your instruction. Too often teachers give the first part of an instruction over the class activity, and then have to repeat it.

Consider your manner. Do not be diffident, implying by phrase or tone that you really rather doubt if anyone is going to obey. One teacher tried to quell a rather bouncy, noisy class by saying in a pleasant but half-hearted voice: 'I'd like you to carry on, if you could, please. All right?' Of course, the class took little notice: and the noise went on.

On the other hand, do not be unnecessarily stern or abrupt. Instruct with firmness but pleasantness. A routine instruction like 'Lead on now' can be warm and said with a smile.

Your instructions will be both more pleasant and more effective if they are, as often as possible, positive rather than negative:

'Make sure you bring a pencil tomorrow'
rather than:
'Don't let's have so many forgotten pencils tomorrow!'

'Be absolutely punctual on Friday'
rather than:
'Don't be so late on Friday.'

'Draw this diagram as neatly as you can'
rather than:
'No messy work in these diagrams.'

Typical of the worst method of giving instructions is the question thrown at the whole class (while they are packing up):

'Has everyone given in their books?'

This produces a plethora of 'Yes' and 'No' responses and causes noisy confusion without helping the teacher actually know who still has to hand their books in. Do not turn instructions into questions. For instance, a class that is about to settle to the task of drawing a diagram may include an unknown number who have not brought the necessary pencils. If the teacher asks generally:

'Anybody need pencils?'

there will be a rush of replies from all over, including the otherwise quite unnecessary negative replies from those who *have* pencils. What is more, there is little chance of actually identifying the ones who need the pencils in the rattle of yes's and no's. Instead, give a positive instruction, identifying those who are being addressed, and requiring hand-showing not calling out, thus:

'Those who have *not* got pencils put your hands up, please.'

This signals that those who have got pencils need not listen further, it avoids all calling out, and it clearly shows the teacher where the pencils are wanted.

Never give a second order until the first has been obeyed. Too often a teacher shows his fear that his first instructions will be ignored by winging a second one on its way, and soon the group are deluged in a plethora of unobeyed instructions.

It is worth practising instructions on your own. Then listen to yourself as you give them in school, and observe the response.

Develop a firm warmth, or a warm firmness

If separate sections of a class need different points explained and practised, it is usually better to postpone the splitting until later, getting both groups to work together initially. This occurs sometimes in practical lessons, often in Music, Science, or Drama. If, for instance, the class are to sing, and half need to learn one line and half the other, teach the whole class both first. In a practical

Science lesson the same applies. If half are to do one thing and half the other, explain both to the whole class first. This is educationally better, as they learn more, and it avoids the boredom of waiting.

If an instruction is very unusual, an advance warning is often helpful. When I wanted a large pupil audience to stand for a minute's silence and think about those who had lost their lives in war as part of a Remembrance Day assembly, I told them what I was going to ask and why first. Then I gave a short simple instruction: 'Now stand, please!'

Using 'the board'

Every good teacher should be a good practitioner of 'the art of the board', which includes the most common black chalkboard, plastic boards, and the various forms of projected images, including the interactive whiteboard.

Despite years of derision about teachers and chalk, the chalkboard or the equivalent felt pen and plastic board remains *the* most valuable aid: the technique is simple, clear, ever-ready, flexible, and unobtrusive. It requires no special black-out, and almost no special preparation. You have to check only that:

> For chalkboards: the surface is clear (layers of chalk dust easily build up and writing is obscured); chalk is to hand, and there is a rubber in good condition (not too hard).

> For plastic boards: the surface has been properly cleaned (smears often linger), suitable felt pens are available and still in good condition, and there is a clean wiper. If you press too hard with most pens the surface becomes permanently discoloured.

> For interactive boards and for all forms of projected images: a pre-lesson check of the controls, the screen well set up at the appropriate angle, and the equipment safely clear of pupil movement.

As with words to the class, the basic rule is simple: think twice before use, but if you are going to use, then do so clearly and forcefully. Either the pupils need to read the message on the board or not. If not, do not distract yourself or them by writing on the board. If they do need to, ensure that what you write can be found (it is not lost in a random corner amongst diagrams and a jumble of jottings), can be read (your writing must be large enough and clear), and can be understood (enigmatic half phrases or dark hints are useless).

If you know that all the pupils should read a section of text, avoid the labour, class time, and strain of reading from the board: have a duplicated sheet ready for distribution to each pupil. Occasionally, prepared headings can be on the board in advance, acting as signposts for the progress of the lesson. Similarly, if new technical terms or difficult concept words are to be key to the lesson, they can be awaiting the class on the board. It is particularly useful for building up ideas and suggestions from the class into a coherent pattern. The teacher's layout of ideas collected thus from the class can certainly be copied by the pupils from the board, but never use it for copying a pre-written text. For this, photocopy and distribute.

An effective occasional variant is to devise an exercise in which the pupils amend the text on display. They really like to do this, and it is an educational way of a pupil sharing her or his thinking with the class, who *see* the idea being formulated. Although awkward, this can be done directly onto the board itself, or onto an OHP transparency. The interactive whiteboard is the best technology for this, and significantly increases the range of options open to the teacher and pupils, making pupil contributions to the text displayed to the whole class really effective.

In the case of black- and whiteboards, always start with a perfectly clear board. Well before the first pupil enters, check that the board is entirely clean and free of smudgy layers of chalk. Some cleaners will do this beautifully, but a pupil will often be a willing and meticulous 'board monitor'. Check that you have a good rubber handy (old cloths are *no* use, and some proprietary rubbers need working in and softening before they will work pleasantly). Check also that there is a modest supply of the chalks or markers you wish to use that morning. (Do not hoard a box full of worn scrap ends – you will only have to scrabble through them.)

Writing on the board

It is possible to talk and write at the same time. The technique is to stand as *close* to the board as possible, with your head facing about 45° away from it. You are thus looking along the board and at a sector of the class. Keeping your feet still, turn to the class fully at each sensible point. Of course, you would never write whole passages on the board with the pupils in the room. Indeed, for the display of an existing text (whether your own or a key quotation) an OHP transparency word-processed in advance is immensely more effective. The use of boards during the lesson is essentially for work in progress, words, phrases, diagrams, which you wish to illustrate spontaneously or you wish to show *changing* (for example, adding suffixes to words). If you stand centrally, you will be forced to write standing in front of your work. If you stand too far away, you will again find that you tend to have your back fully to the class. Keep close and to one side of your work.

Layout on the board

The key to clarity is not so much the details of your handwriting as the disposition of your writing on the board. Establish from the first an imaginary grid on the board to give you clear columns for your writing, with real or merely visualized margins. If it is a wide board, you may need two columns. Other kinds of work would best be laid out in, perhaps, three columns. To write straight across a wide board is unwise as it is difficult to keep the line satisfactorily horizontal, and it is difficult for the pupils' eyes to carry right across the long line.

Establish conventions about the use of space on the boards. It may be that you will want to use one section always for the date, another for the instructions for the work in hand, and yet another for the homework instructions. It is often wise to reserve a section for a list of the vocabulary which you draw up during the period. There is nothing more frustrating for a pupil than to have to scan a jumbled board for a word that the teacher put up only a few moments ago and which is vital to the work in hand. I have seen some teachers flinging words in any corner of the board, overlapping, jammed up in a congested corner, and weaving through old lines and bits and pieces. If you are likely to add words or phrases, start a column and keep to it.

Some things should be put on a board or prepared for the projector on a screen in advance: particularly diagrams, maps, lists of questions, or notes. Not only is it too difficult for most teachers to make a decent job of such work on the board without concentrating single-mindedly, but also it is unwise to get in a situation where you have to face the board for a sustained piece of drawing or writing. Particularly inept is to have to end a tricky question and answer or discussion question by a great wadge of writing on the board. Instead of the pupils being able to get straight into their work, they have to wait until you have finished the first piece of writing, and even then your bobbing figure and jogging arm are distractions for most. Furthermore, just when your eye and presence are needed for settling the group into the new mood of a different style of work, you are distracted by the needs of draughtsmanship. However, the interactive whiteboard and digitalized materials have huge potential, which is complementary to the blackboard, allowing the ready retention of alternative texts and their easy selection and display.

There are three possible solutions:

(a) issue photocopied sheets ready prepared keeping them a secret on your desk until the dramatic moment, and then issuing them briskly;

(b) have the material ready prepared on a ready-focused OHP, to be switched on at the appropriate moment (it is essential to have the transparency on the projector and focused before the lesson);

(c) prepare the material on a section of the board before the lesson, preferably a section which can be covered (by a sliding panel, revolving section, or roller board) until you want to reveal it. This revelation can be forceful and effective: it is a device as old as any, but is still very useful.

Compared with the first and second solutions, both of which utilize material which can be stored and used again, the use of the board for extensive written material is, of course, very time consuming.

Handwriting

Your actual handwriting requires care: a firmly simplified hand is best, with no lavish loops. A constant firm pressure to produce a strong impression is essential. The stance while writing needs practice. Despite the advice on the previous page, it is necessary to be able to keep an eye on the class whilst writing. With a traditional blackboard this requires a position facing *across* the board, so that the head can turn to the class whilst the arm is still raised. With a free-standing board or one projecting well from the wall, I find it best to stand against the side of the board. It is worth remembering that it is found by most people to be very difficult to write much below chest height. On a fixed board, therefore, regard the lowest band as unusable.

Do not 'print' (that is, use upper case throughout) except for special purposes. The configuration of lower case letters with the ascenders and descenders, makes them considerably easier to read (witness the style of motorway signs).

Coloured chalks or pens are helpful if used skilfully. Eschew the pale colours as they cannot be seen easily. Yellow and red are your two best allies. Diagrams and maps apart, for they obviously have their own logic and demands, use white chalk or black pen as your basic colours. Do not pick any old colour so that the pupils have yellow sometimes and blue at others. If you indulge in this random scatter, you will have sacrificed the effect of the deliberate use of colour. Save your alternative colours for such explanatory purposes as:

> breaking up parts of words;
> underlining;
> grouping by lines or brackets;
> special lists;
> differentiating.

Again, establish conventions suitable to your subject, your class, and you, and then keep to them. That way colour will work for you.

The overhead projector

Well set up and well used, the OHP is an admirable, technologically superior, version of the two forms of boards: the image can be stronger, the display can not only be prepared in advance but can be prepared photographically, avoiding copying time and sharpening quality; photographs and professional drawings can be used; the image can be changed virtually instantaneously; it is very easy for building up jottings mid-lesson – and very significantly there should be no need to look round at the screen, and the teacher's eyes can be communicating with the class throughout. Unfortunately few schools have OHPs in classrooms with built-in screens ready for regular use. Lighting is often difficult, though full blackout is not required. The fact is that for illustrations the OHP is marvellous, for example, old paintings in History, detailed diagrams in Science, original designs and photographs of the finished item in D&T. When the image teaches, OHP transparencies are superb.

Conclusion

'Chalk and talk' has become a stupidly exaggerated pejorative phrase. So many teachers have learnt to despise any kind of teaching that could be labelled by such a tag that the profession is not retaining and improving its presentational skills. A good speaker will not necessarily be a good teacher, but the ability to communicate well in speaking is still one of the central skills of a teacher. It is curious how at a time when we are more than ever aware of the need to develop the speech of pupils, we are making them do more of their learning from reading, and less from the spoken voice and the interchange of question and answer. Similarly, the various kinds of boards and screens with both projected texts and handwritten ones and using appropriate images are essential for a whole variety of lessons in a whole variety of subjects. I recommend that the pejorative implications are forgotten, and that you become as skilful as possible with the modern versions of 'chalk and talk'. The teacher in tutor period or course lesson *is* a 'performer' for part of the time, putting across with voice, expression, gesture, and display a reaction, an instruction, or the content of ideas and concepts. Reading, display, and oral skills are part of the craft.

7

The rhythm of a lesson

A lesson has to be organized as a sequence arranged in time, and the pattern of the learning activities must fit the curriculum aims, the pupils, and the stretch of time available. The law in England and Wales about the National Curriculum is far more flexible than many realize, and even the Literacy and Numeracy strategies for Key Stage Three are not statutory requirements. The content of a *school's* curriculum has to include the NC contents, but the school itself decides the division into subject courses and can add to the content.[19]

The rhythm of the teaching activities in a lesson is an important factor under the control of the teacher. Even lessons that seem to organize themselves, such as a double Science lesson with a major practical activity, in fact require their time-sequence planning. The pupil in a school is in a time-structured environment and expects that the component elements of the day should similarly be time structured. There is no escape from this demand for a use of time which is complete, intensive, and varied. The pupil is stimulated by a good use of time, and bored and irritated by bad use. For instance, a hurried change of activity near the end of a lesson with insufficient time for the changeover or the activity itself irritates the pupils and wastes time. A lesson is a presentation, however much pupil participation there is, and its rhythm and pace are part of the enjoyment. When a pupil declares later in the day 'That was a good lesson!', it is frequently the pacing of the lesson which has created the feeling of satisfaction. As the TTA's definition of Standards for QTS puts it, qualified teachers should ensure that:

> 'They organize and manage teaching and learning time effectively.'[1]

119

The pattern of a lesson

'Lesson planning' will eventually become an instinctive activity, even one that can continue at the back of your mind while you are doing other things. As you get more experienced and your repertoire of lesson activities grows, you will find it easier to select and to arrange almost unconsciously, only occasionally needing to write the details down. In the early days, and whenever you are on unfamiliar territory, it is worth writing down the activities and the time to be devoted to them.

The key to this planning, however, is not the writing down. Many written lesson plans look good at first glance, but are worse than useless in their inaccuracy of conception. The key is the ability to think through a lesson in advance, as it were, to preview rapidly the entire stretch of time. This is an imaginative feat that takes in the learning activities, the nature of the room and its facilities, the pupil group and its key individuals, and the occasion of the day. In some ways, teachers of Science are helped by their burdensome equipment demands, which force them to specify their precise needs to the lab technicians in advance, and then to visualize the whole lesson. Such an approach is required, however, by all teachers. (On p. 124 I give an example of a skeleton lesson plan.)

The starting point is a review of the range of activities:

- *who?* whole-class, small groups, triads, pairs, individual?
- *how chosen?* self, arbitrary (for example, alphabetical), friendship groups, gender, special interests, attainment?
- *what?* listening, discussing, reading, researching a range of sources, designing, constructing, role play, individual or group presentation, investigations, writing, checking each other's work?

Timing

Then you need to consider the length of the lessons: 30-, 35-, 40-, 50-, or 60-minute periods are all to be found in different schools. Whereas some schools use double (or triple) periods only for 'practical' subjects, others have an extensive use of longer sessions for very many if not most subjects. Sometimes whole or half days are fitted into the term. Obviously, a double 40-minute lesson gives a period of 80 minutes. This is a very long stretch of time and needs careful apportioning.

There is some evidence that teachers use shorter sessions more intensively than longer periods. Thus, the longer teaching periods can be reduced in effectiveness by a drop in the intensity of the use of the time, and a consequent increase in pupil boredom.

The effective length of time will obviously depend on the pattern of pupil movement. If, as with younger classes in some secondary schools, the teacher moves to the class, and if, for instance, the period is the second single of two, the teacher can work to virtually the whole of the clock time. If, as is more common, the pupils move to the teacher's room, there has to be a reasonable reduction for movement. You should work out the effective length of the lesson, and then consider how it can be broken down. It is important to think always of what the pupils will be *doing* at a given moment, and to visualize how one activity joins to the next.

Shape of the lesson

Every lesson needs a shape, and its shape is made up of the units of time into which it is divided. The relationship between these units creates the rhythm. I do not want to over-elaborate this way of looking at teaching, but I would stress the immense value of rhythmic variety. You can represent a typical lesson rhythm diagramatically in this way:

(*a* i) Conventional use of double periods:

exposition	activity	conclusion

(*b* i) Sometimes there are two preludes:

work handed back	exposition or stimulus	activity	conclusion

My comment would be that both these are acceptable patterns, but both have their faults, and neither should be overused. Certainly, (a i) is far too often the basic rhythm of Science lesson after lesson, and (b i) is too often the standard pattern of innumerable English lessons. Both have their objections. For a double period, the central activity in (a i) is very often too long in relation to the range of activities involved, and in proportion to the sandwich of exposition and conclusion. (b i) suffers from two starting units which are too similar: it is frequently nearly impossible to get the pupils into the activity after such a repeated false start. As a variant on (a i) I would suggest:

(a ii)

initial activity	explanation and exposition	main activity	final summary

In this case there is a brief introductory activity ready laid out with instructions to start the lesson and *precede* the main exposition, which is now reinforced by some activity in advance. (This may, of course, be a practical activity, or it may involve writing as a precursor to the lesson.) Yet a further alternative to (a i) would be this:

(a iii)

main activity	explanation	writing

In which case the main activity has to be entered into cold, presuming that directions and apparatus are clear enough for this to be possible. In pattern (a iii) the writing occupies a final stretch of time of perhaps twenty minutes, and is designed for pondering the activity, reflecting on it, and letting its conclusions sink in. (I think that far too often pupils rush straight out to the playground from an activity, without an opportunity for it to 'register'.) This final section will be used for clearing up and putting away, as well as providing an opportunity for the teacher to go over points quietly with one or two pupils.

As an occasional alternative to (*b* i) I should offer:

(*b* ii)

exposition or stimulus	activity	work handed back

This avoids the problem of the double start, although it risks too long an activity section for it to be suitable for all occasions. It would work if the balance between the three units was right. A further variation is:

(*b* iii)

exposition or stimulus	initial activity	work handed back	main activity

This allows the lesson to be 'played out' with the main activity, which is especially suitable if it is to lead straight into homework (but see my point about dating on p. 58). Presuming that you *want* a group handing-back of work on this occasion (there may well be times when you would prefer to hand it back individually with a quiet private word), I have suggested as a variation that this is inserted *after* the main activity has been started. Such a break can, of course, be jerkily irritating. However, it can sometimes be effective and justified. I have, for instance, often noticed how many times a run of work is actually broken by the teacher's interpolated comments. If you do this, capitalize on the break, make something of it, and draw some relevant points from the work being handed back.

Whatever your views on the six patterns I have just sketched, I hope that you will agree that there are a number of variations of pace and rhythm, and that lessons should not settle monotonously into only one pattern. The variations should be used both for functional relevance to the nature of the learning activity, and also for the sheer value of variety.

Lesson planning

Here is an example of pre-lesson plan jottings. This was to be a Maths lesson on arrow diagrams, with a number of sections. The double lesson was after break, which ended nominally at 11.15. The times on the right are finishing times to help the teacher see roughly when each section should be completed. You will notice that there were five minutes in hand, as the final bell went at 12.35. (By the way, never keep a class in except as a punishment: they resent being late out.)

On the board in advance:

starter instruction			
key words (ringed in teacher's book)			
my arrow diagram			
family tree			
Timing (2x40=80)		time:	finished by:
Starter on paper		5	11.20
Intro: 'What are we doing?'		5	11.25
New work on board		5	11.30
Silent study of p.103 a,b,c		15	11.45
Oral questions and answers and explanation of these		15	12.00
Written exercise p.105		20	12.20
Final summary and questions		10	12.30
		75	
	therefore five minutes spare		
N.B. collect books			

Of course, the wise teacher does not keep rigidly to a preplanned shape. She will judge the mood of the class and the response to the learning activity. She may well continue a successful activity for considerably longer than she had planned; she certainly may abandon intended sections; she may have 'reserve' activities available; she may even insert a spontaneous activity. Such flexibility is obviously necessary as the success or even the timing of a part of a lesson cannot be gauged fully in advance.

Yet this flexibility should not be too great. If, for instance, an explanation to the class is proving more difficult than anticipated, and therefore taking longer, it could well be wiser, nevertheless, to keep to the plan for the lesson, sum up the explanation achieved so far, and leave it for this occasion, returning to the topic in the next lesson. This is not always possible – for a fair understanding of the topic may be essential for the remainder of that session's learning activity. However, it can be disastrous to abandon the plan and plug away at the explanation, thus destroying the texture of time.

A contrasting example would be a lesson that was to have had in it a limited period of writing. The teacher finds that when it comes to the time at which he had planned to break off the writing and read some fresh material to the class, play an audio cassette, or present a summary, all the pupils are miraculously engrossed in their writing, and it seems a tragedy to break the concentration. On such an occasion he may be wise to capitalize on the flow of energy, scrap the next planned activity, and let the writing continue. However, I should caution against too great a flexibility even here. The extra time you can offer on this occasion is probably insufficient for the work to be completed; if you abandon your plan and allow the writing to continue, you might well find it petering out before the end of the lesson, with an awkward gap left.

Finally, the teacher, as much as preacher or the television performer, does well to remember that the customer is often better satisfied if he or she is left wanting more. Better a class saying 'Why can't we go on writing?' than one desperately longing for the writing to end.

One of the most common slips is to be 'caught by the bell' – that is to be midstream in a pupil activity, oral exposition, or video when the forgotten lesson-change signal cuts in. However the pressure of the lesson warps the intended plan, it is possible and necessary to wind up and 'give back' the lesson in time for a summation, tidying up, and supervised, orderly departure.

There is something to be said for fixed and regular routines for the start of a lesson: after all, you cannot properly give the pupils any instructions until they have joined you, and a regular expectation of what they should start doing is in effect a carried-over instruction. Thus they could know to go to their places, take out their Diary and folder, and so on. One technique that combines routine clarity with the possibility of variety is to have an activity set out on OHP or board. Then try to vary the start: too many lessons have an absolute ritual of teacher's oral start, explaining and exhorting. Occasionally you can deploy a brief reading, a series of OHP pictures, question and answer session, pupil-prepared presentation, or straight into a piece of writing.

Pupils also need to know where the lesson is going, how much of the time they will have in which to choose their own activities, how long they will spend on a piece of research in History, or what proportion of the period will be devoted to full-class question and answer in a language lesson. For too many pupils, most lessons are a more or less exciting mystery tour, in which they never know how long they are going to be at one activity before they are set down or whipped off for another. The teacher needs to establish 'signposts' in a lesson, sometimes even having a clear note of the lesson objectives displayed on the board.

The introduction should vividly and clearly share the lesson's objectives with the pupils:

- 'Today we are going to explore the technology of our school building, and work out what materials and techniques it uses.'
- 'In this lesson we are going to study when and why writers use the hyphen, and how it shows the connection of words and thus the meaning.'

Planning activity

It is the oldest and one of the most sensible of teachers' sayings that pupils must have something to *do*. This is so for two complementary reasons: in the first place, we can all learn effectively by doing (especially if the actions are preceded and reinforced by an explanation and by the pupils' own verbalization and reflection). In the second place, pupils enjoy doing things, and on the whole do not much enjoy listening. One study of a large sample of lessons showed that in English and some other

Humanities lessons 38% of the time was spent listening. If this is of well-presented expositions it can be both beneficial and enjoyable. However, much of the time may be filled by awkwardly expressed answers by pupil after pupil. I have observed as much as half of a 50-minute lesson taken up in this way. The teacher was confusing checking whether the pupils understood with educating the class as a whole. It is insufferably tedious for a pupil to sit in a class whilst 'Sir' asks pupil after pupil a question and each fumbles for an answer. This is *not* discussion or debate and is not an activity of interest to or value for the other members of the class.

The experienced teacher makes sure that every lesson offers ample opportunity for activity, and that there is ample activity for each pupil, whatever his ability. These activities should be cunningly placed in the lesson. For instance, I have already suggested that there should often be an initial activity as the first section, however short, of a lesson. The purpose of this initial activity may be to get the pupils thinking, for instance, or to raise questions in their minds. Thus its full understanding may depend on a later synthesis and explanation.

If there is to be a long stretch of activities, it is important that the directions (on board, screen, or worksheet) should be *clear enough for the majority of the class to move on without having to ask questions*. There is nothing more ruinous of the rhythm of a lesson than the constipated jerkiness created by pupils who cannot move ahead without further help.

In mixed-ability classes, especially, it is obviously important that each sequence of activities should start with ones that are simple enough for all, and, conversely, that there are others difficult enough to stretch the most able, and sufficient of them. Never underestimate the pleasure, satisfaction, and educational value which pupils get from satisfactorily completing an action, *however simple*. This is especially true of techniques like certain measurements in Maths, aspects of map reading, movements in Dance, or experiments in Science.

It is worth spending time thinking up activities to help *towards* the teaching of a fact or a skill. It is a frequent mistake to want the pupils to learn the real point too early: a set of 'limbering up' activities is most valuable. For instance, how would you help the pupils to learn about contours or paragraphs? Or how would you prepare them for measuring temperatures? In both cases a mere identifying exercise is a valuable starter. In the first case, to 'trace over in a brown pencil the contour lines on this map' (specially drawn for simplicity). In the second example, have the pupils mark with a red pencil all the paragraph indentations in a reproduced page or two from a printed book. In the third, have them look at duplicated reproductions of a thermometer scale, and write in the scale points. The art of teaching includes the art of devising quick and straightforward activities.

Variety is as important in the activities devised as it is in the overall rhythm of the lesson. For instance, try to avoid offering young secondary pupils an interminable diet of worksheets, so that the activities are similar not merely throughout the lesson, but also from lesson to lesson. This soon palls – especially if, as too often happens, your colleagues are similarly addicted to worksheets in other subject courses. 'Individual learning', far from being a panacea, can be a yawning bore – it relies on good reading, good motivation, and good behaviour. It gives insufficient teacher feedback to the majority of pupils, and leaves dozens with their hands up for long sections of the day. I have seen pupils with their hands up for twenty minutes at a time.

Stillness and movement

For most lessons there are sections which are more or less still and quiet and sections which are more or less active and noisy. One of the arts of patterning is to vary these elements. In the early years of adolescence – indeed, I should say right through to the end of compulsory schooling – pupils can rarely take too much of one or the other. The mixture needs to be varied. In a Humanities lesson, discussion, question and answer, cutting and sticking activities are clearly times of noise and activity, whereas reading, writing, or various kinds of worksheets are basically still and quiet. In Science, there is an obvious similar distinction between group experiments, which thrive on bustle and conversation, and noting down, measuring, and writing, which require peace. In languages, there is the contrast between oral work and writing.

My first advice is to exaggerate rather than to blur these distinctions. The variety of the rhythm will be less attractive if the activities are indistinguishable, and if there is always dead hush and stillness (a rare fault this, however!) or a general wash of noise and movement throughout everything (a much more common situation). Part of the value of the still sections is precisely their contrast with the more active ones. Play the variations with a musician's skill. Sometimes have your stillness for a long central section; at other times start with a calm, still section; and at other times make your coda a final fifteen minutes of stillness.

To open with a still, and therefore settling, section is often the easiest for a young teacher who finds the task of getting quiet out of noise more difficult. It is surprising, therefore, that it is not more often used. I recommend that there should be 'still' work to hand as pupils come in, with the work on the desk, directions given personally to them as they enter, and the instructions confirmed by a clear direction already on a board. Start a double period with twenty minutes of that – rather than the movement of handing back some writing with your oral comments.

Above all, pattern the variations of stillness and movement, of quiet and of voices, as a deliberate part of the rhythm of the lesson, for the rhythm of a lesson can support the teaching aim and help the learner.

Summing up

Almost every learning session benefits from a final 'summing up' – what can be thought of as 'the plenary'. Apart from anything else, pupils who have been obliged to spend, say, an hour and twenty minutes in a room are happier if they are reminded before leaving of what they have achieved. They need, as it were, the final signpost or arrival board. At a carefully judged point near the end, usually gain the attention of the whole group. This may be the very last task before the clock shows that it is time to go; it may be prior to 'clearing up'; it may, less often, be the penultimate activity, and the lesson session may end with a final fifteen minutes of quiet activity. The teacher, having gained the undivided attention of the pupils, should briskly, and with praise if this is at all justifiable, run over what has been learnt or otherwise achieved:

> 'Today almost everyone has completed their long story, and we seem to have an impressive collection already.'

> 'Now we have really got that point about contour lines quite clear.'

> 'You've all done valuable work from the cards today. This means we've all learnt something about how we measure heat.'

It is obviously important not to use the summing up to embark on a fresh lesson. However, it is usually possible to pick up the salient features of the session, highlight the contributions of a few members of the group, and as it were, give the group back their achievement so that they can feel something has been achieved. This rounding-off must not be allowed to become a mere empty routine, but usually it is a wise final shot – especially in a lesson which has been largely occupied with individual assignments. On many occasions the pupils should participate in this, either in brief question and answer, or in a prepared statement. Where a key concept has been explored, such as 'circuit' in electricity or 'environment' in geography, it can be very valuable to have a pithy, eloquent, and memorable summary phrase. Try not to dismiss the class amidst only a plethora of tidying-up business and behavioural exhortations. Lessons are not *about* being quiet and tidy (except for some tutorial sessions on those themes) and the last memory for the pupil should be of the core of the lesson content, not the trivia of its procedures. The teacher should endeavour through the summing up to enable the pupils consciously to define what they have got from the lesson and, very importantly, consider what they have made of that content.

Fillers

Although they will not be used often, an experienced teacher has a store of 'fillers' which can be slipped into the last five or ten minutes of a lesson. A lesson must end if not with a bang at least with a definite note. Too many drift away with a whimper. If it seems likely that there is to be time left, instead of stretching the material out desperately, compress it. Keeping an eye on the clock, draw the threads together earlier than planned; go through your clearing up and closing routine briskly and energetically, and then, with the lesson completely finished and five minutes to go, launch briefly into your 'filler'.

This can be based on old material from your subject presented in the form of question and answer, or a game, one side of the class against the other. It can be based on puzzles derived from your subject, or on the etymology of words which are part of your subject. This is an excellent moment for a brief reading of a poem, incident, or description; one that you know well and which in some way links with the class's interests. It is a good moment for each to jot down a couple of words in answer to some question. This is even a time when some aspect of school routine, future planning, or class business can be introduced. Indeed it may be time for a disconnected activity based on words, number, or general knowledge for an intelligent, brisk ending.

Two warnings: do not use 'fillers' too often – they lose their function; and keep them very brief: like a pre-faded track on a television programme, their climax should precisely synchronize with the clock.

The rhythm of a sequence of lessons

I have been speaking of the rhythm of a lesson. It is important to stress that I am not recommending that there is one 'ideal' rhythm for a group. Despite my emphasis on routines and procedures for a class, it is vital that there is rhythmic variety between lessons. If you meet a class, for instance, for two doubles in a week, you should sense the need to vary the pattern, perhaps having five basic patterns, four of which you use in every fortnight. A class, such as Maths, which meets for five or more periods each week, might well benefit from one session each week having a fixed and routine pattern – it might be a test, a silent reading period, a presentation, or a serious story. Such a 'fixed feast' gives the teacher a respite from planning and the pupils a known resting point. But the other four sessions need varying so that the tempo is neither known nor repetitive.

Further, an individual lesson will to some extent be influenced by that lesson's position in the day and the week. For instance, the first lesson after an assembly in most schools has a slightly varied time of starting; those preceding lunch need a strictly timed ending; last lessons in the afternoon need especial care.

One of the major skills of a teacher is a highly developed inner clock, which is used to pace the activities, not in a merely mechanical way, but in a subtle, almost aesthetic pattern. The recommendations of the National Literacy and Numeracy hours need not be mechanically followed, though advice such as the use of a 'plenary' is often helpful. Rhythmic variety and suitability contribute to effective teaching.

The sequence of the year

Pupils need to know that they are going somewhere. It is therefore wise to take them into your confidence with the plan of the year, how it links with what has gone before, and what it leads on to. This is especially so in light of National Curriculum programmes of study and SATs. If possible, create opportunities for choice within this framework so that pupils have a hand in their own destiny. Give them a printed overall plan of the year and its broad coverage of topics, so that they see an overview of the curriculum plan and have some idea of what they should achieve and the route they will take. Create as much variety of texture as you can over the year, so that week after week is not an interminable routine. Mark out clearly any stages reached, and make it clear that progress is being made.

Inevitably, I have spoken about what the teacher does, and I have described situations from the teacher's point of view. Of course, it is the pupil's learning that matters, and in the end the test is not what you have *taught*, but what the pupil has actually *learned*. A teacher will develop ways of picking up the clues of expressions, remarks, actions, and questions to gauge how well the pupils have learnt. He or she will supplement this by deliberate assessment procedures, whether they are a simple question in a Science lesson, a rapid check of words learnt in a Modern Language lesson, a quiz, or a more definite test. Sciences, Languages, and Maths need frequent modest assessment procedures, not primarily for grading the pupils, but to provide a feedback to the teacher. From this feedback the teacher will both vary the learning experiences and give feedback to the pupils so that they have a sense of progress – a necessary feeling.

All schools have overall assessment policies, which incorporate the statutory national demands for standard assessment, and ensures that those external assessments are fully *used* by the school, not merely grudgingly followed because the statutory regulations require it. External assessment is an essential referencing procedure, allowing the individual teacher and the school to put other more informal assessment against nationwide criteria. Thus, pupil feedback, reporting to parents, curriculum and planning, and school action over 'at-risks' groups can all be helped.

'Critical incidents' such as formal assessment, reporting to parents, option choices, and examination entries are times of extra work for pupils in the school year. The course teacher has to plan a shape that is derived from the curriculum plan but also takes these external forces into account. Also to be considered is your own year as an individual: any absence (perhaps because of in-service Professional Development), appraisal, the school's professional development days, and the high points of curriculum planning work and reporting to parents. As far as planning can be so detailed, you would wish to avoid clashing the most stressful parts of the school year with the peak demands of the work from your classes: agonizing between giving time in the evening to writing reports for parents or marking the current pile of pupils' books.

8

Preparing yourself

You will hear often the need to 'prepare your lessons', and I have extended this to preparing a range of aspects of the room and the routine. Finally, though, there are ways in which a teacher needs to prepare her- or himself more personally. In this section I shall suggest how your skill in the classroom needs to be supported by personal preparation.

It has always been realized, and, indeed, even enjoyed, that one of the key aspects of the profession of teaching in schools is that one has to find a range of ways of continuing to develop one's interests, specialisms, the needs of the pupils, and the changing expectations and style of society. A school and LEA should have well-established ways of fostering 'Continuous Professional Development'. However, for this to be effective and rewarding for you as an individual it requires your own commitment, involvement, research, and intervention. The TTA standards include a powerful summary of this, requiring of qualified teachers that:

> 'They are able to improve their own teaching, by evaluating it, learning from the effective practice of others and from evidence. They are motivated and able to take increasing responsibility for their own professional development.'[1]

Using the school

To work from a position of strength it is necessary for you to feel completely sure of the school context into which your own work fits. Some schools are fairly good at making their routines and procedures clear through explicit documentation and briefing sessions, but it must be admitted that this is one of the weaker aspects of school organization, though one considerably improved by the development of Induction Programmes.

Most schools produce a 'Staff Handbook', and other organizational documentation. Obviously you will study it carefully. Some procedures may be arbitrary; more have probably grown out of particular points of the locality, building, organizational structure, timetabling scheme, and so on. It is wise to assume that there is a reason for everything, and to find out that reason if possible. Later, you may wish to join in discussions to modify or substantially change those procedures. However, whilst they stand, operate them punctiliously. If all the teachers in the school work to the same procedures, each is supporting the other.

Soon after your appointment, arrange a visit to the school to find out as much as you can. Very important indeed is to meet and ensure you get to know your Induction Tutor if you are a NQT. Important as the 'Career Entry Profile' document is, many have criticized it as inadequate and I recommend your taking additional personal papers of your career and interests.

Other key figures to get to know closely are your Head of Department and for your tutorial pastoral responsibility the Head of Year, Year Co-ordinator, or Head of House for whom you will be working. From your Head of Department you will want a scheme of work, copies of the main resources, including textbooks in particular, with which you will be working, and details of the classes and the timetable.

You will want to find out the communication and responsibility pattern of the school. What is the role of each of the senior staff? Therefore, to whom do you refer what? What is the procedure for supporting you if you have difficulties in the classroom? What supervisory duties will you be asked to undertake (such as playground supervision in break), and who will guide you in them?

Make sure you are told about the school's support staff, who they are, and what are their functions, for example: Is there a professional librarian? Who is head of the general office and what responsibilities does she or he carry? What is the correct title of the person responsible for the building and its general equipment – often called 'Premises Manager'? Where is he or she based, and what is the range of her or his responsibilities? Are there any specialized technicians in your subject department, and for what can you ask their help? Also, are there any school-wide technicians, for ICT, sound equipment, off-air TV recording, graphic design, or reprographics?

Your department team should give you specialist support in your subject teaching. You can expect to discuss all your problems with the Head of Department, from pupils to equipment, from rooms to routines. Make sure that you put your worries to him or her as early as possible. If you are unlucky enough to work under an unusual Head of Department who does not offer this kind of help, turn to your Induction Tutor instead.

Watch other colleagues at work, especially those in different disciplines. An English teacher, for instance, has a great deal to learn from the techniques of exposition of a Maths teacher; a Humanities teacher can often learn from the handling of practical and group work in a Science lesson; a Science teacher may learn much from the structured discussion techniques of an English teacher; many specialists can learn from the typical PE teacher's methods of settling groups and giving instructions.

As a NQT you will often turn to your Induction Tutor, appointed by the Headteacher under national requirements to assist you and others establish yourselves in the profession and confirm your QTS. A good Induction Tutor will have a programme of informal discussions, and give you the opportunity to meet with others to analyse professional problems.

Conserving energy

Learn to pace your day and your weeks. The great Shakespearian actor, John Gielgud, said that the key to playing King Lear was to pace the part, so that he had sufficient physical and emotional energy in reserve for the later climaxes. The same is true of teaching. You will have a large number of periods and tutorial sessions to teach each week. You cannot afford to prepare too many of those in great detail: you will not have time. You cannot allow too many of them to involve great vocal strain: you will not have any voice left. You cannot work too hard in too many: you will be exhausted before the end of each day.

Even small matters, like getting to your class in good time and having any handout worksheets ready, save that rush and tension that can be tiring in itself and can also make the lesson more tiring for you. For instance, turning to write a point on the board or screen and finding it is full and needs cleaning adds to your tiredness. Preparation of all aspects, the room, all learning materials, and books to hand back reduces your use of energy and your worry. These are small points but they add up.

For much of this book I have been inevitably concerned with the individual learning session, a period or double period. Similarly, the young teacher's concerns tend to focus on the problems of managing a single session. To a degree this is wise, for the first target is clearly to become proficient at leading a successful lesson. However, in time it becomes clear that the real problem is not the individual session, but the run of lessons over a month or half a term. This is what creates the pupils' learning experiences. More immediately, though, teachers need to consider the longer sequence from their own point of view. They must learn to conserve their energy if they are to give of their best consistently. Too often, young teachers find it difficult to cope because of frayed nerves and flagging energy. Obviously we all expect to be tired at the end of a week's work, but if the tiredness is welling up mid-week and midday and seriously hampering effective handling of the classroom, then something is wrong with your pacing of the week. You have to work hard and plan to keep fresh. You cannot afford to get overtired.

Apart from the need to try to plan term-time weekday evenings carefully, it is wise to try to phase those lessons that are difficult to prepare and those which are difficult and physically more exhausting to deliver so that they do not clash with each other or with major school events that put pressure on you.

Being in training

A great deal depends on inner calm. It is almost as if a teacher needs to be in physical and psychological training for the classroom. If you are tired, worried, torn apart with inner stress, or hectic from rushing, it is extremely difficult to keep your cool in the classroom.

A group of adolescents is both demanding and challenging to be with, whatever classroom mode you are using. You will not be able to cope with them if you cannot cope with yourself.

It would be impertinent to offer advice about evenings and weekends in a book about the teacher's management of the classroom. However, it is a very real fact that the dynamic of a teacher's working year is very different from that of, say, an office manager. It is no good the teacher merely moaning about the awful stresses of teaching and how no other job is as wearing. Success in the classroom depends, amongst other things, upon realizing fairly precisely in what ways a teacher's lot is a *different* one, and taking those differences into account.

The pattern of teaching: responsibility

There are really two crucial differences: one is the pattern of responsibility and the other is the pattern of time. Young teachers who have listened carefully to lectures and seminars about 'the gifted and talented' and 'children with difficulties' and have considered conscientiously the learning needs of children nevertheless find the shock of actual responsibility for them very great indeed. It is, in fact, an open-ended responsibility, for the needs of children are so great that there is never a clear stopping point where you can mentally tick a task off as 'completed'. Indeed, the more sensitive and conscientious you are, the more aware you will be of the inevitable sense of failure and the more appalled by the never-ending vista of further needs.

This nagging responsibility is quite unlike many a professional or commercial responsibility, which is for some part of a process: if the individual carries out his task skilfully, others take the final responsibility. In those jobs, the individual can hand his task on and dispatch it from his mind also. Not so the teacher. This constant sense of unfulfilled responsibility and further needs of the pupils drives some teachers to cynicism, others to frantically continuous political action, others to almost neurotic preparation of teaching materials, and others to despair.

You must cope with it by working hard when you are working, but learn to switch off and take up your private pursuits at other times. Overcome by the emotional impact of the open-ended responsibilities, too many teachers sit and brood, chewing over the pupils' needs, and wasting time and nervous energy regretting that they cannot do more for them. You must be able to switch off.

The pattern of teaching: time

The pattern of time needs reflecting upon also. It is not a fact that over the year as a whole the conscientious teacher puts in more hours than an opposite number in some other comparable occupation. What is true, however, is that that time is put in more unevenly, and this needs planning for. University life, with its even longer holidays, lateish mornings, and comparatively relaxed days, is very poor training for the school-teaching week. The number of days in the year in which you do not have to attend school is fairly high, but the amount of work that you need to get through in a teaching week is huge and very intense – and it will not wait for attention later!

Many teachers have worked in other occupations and find the intensity of a day's sequence of lessons a considerable strain at first. The intensity of the day is very great. Consider the gradual way a Monday morning gets going in some offices: a number of people come in rather later; there is less work waiting in the in-trays; coffee breaks can be a trifle longer and the weekend discussed; even the lunch hour can be extended. I find many teachers, on the other hand, suffer from Sunday-evening pangs, as a creeping worry about the next morning's work starts filling up the back of the mind. Preparations for the week's work loom ahead, and are frequently started too late, or pushed aside. Either way, and even if the work has actually been done, it is difficult not to be vaguely depressed about the inadequacy and at the same time vaguely resentful about the loss of weekend time.

There is no formula that can work for all, but the prospective teacher needs to realize that the price of being demanded in school for only so many days in the year and so many hours within those days is a very heavy load during that time, with the immediate subject course and tutorial needs bruising against longer-term curriculum planning and materials preparation. Many teachers suffer from the 'teacher evening': 'I'm too tired to do anything, even relax.'

Before term

Before the new term it is worth investing time in seven kinds of preparation:

1 Get to know the school building, key support staff, and the support facilities such as library, photocopying, receptionist, premises management, and clerical arrangements.
2 Find out about the school structure and procedures, and your department and syllabus and how it fits into the whole-school curriculum.
3 Prepare your classroom.
4 Find out about the pupils you will be teaching, and who are their tutors.
5 Prepare your registers (including checking 'known as' names and pronunciation).
6 Prepare learning materials and equipment, and at least some worksheets.
7 Especially establish your working relationship with your Induction Tutor.

Conclusion

For many years there has been a very strong emphasis on the 'subject' specialism. This has contributed a great deal to the secondary school and its impact. However, the curriculum development that has come with it has tended to lead teachers to undervalue general teaching skills, and to over-rely on expertise in a particular subject area and on suitability of 'material'. The legal requirements of the National Curriculum (discussed on p. 119) were not intended to and should not be allowed to drive out the wider range of 'cross-curricular' themes. The conventional wisdom is still that if you have prepared your lesson properly and have well-chosen material, discipline problems will not arise. When despite care, time, invention, and commitment the pupils misbehave the teacher feels confused and wrongly self-critical.

In this book I have emphasized that there are general teaching skills which are applicable to most subject course and tutorial work, to most lesson schemes, and in most schools. These are, furthermore, *school* teaching skills, and essential to the particular learning conditions of secondary schools, however they may have changed. The aspects of 'craft' that I have outlined emphatically refer to all sections of the curriculum and barely change whatever the larger political reorganizations of school government.

There is, of course, no simple answer, no single remedy, and certainly no complete success. With some situations a range of remedies has to be simultaneously applied, and the most that can be hoped for is a partial success. When a teacher is having difficulty, the problems often seem so great that he or she would very much like the whole burden to disappear quietly. It does not, though. What is more, the longer you carry it as a vast amorphous problem, the heavier it becomes as a burden. The only hope is to take it to pieces and see where improvements can be made. Work at the details section by section.

You will often feel you have succeeded, but disappointments will also be fairly frequent. There will also be very encouraging times when pupils show how much they have advanced, demonstrating understanding, knowledge, and skills of which you can feel proud. I know only too well that some people could conscientiously apply all the ideas I have given and yet not get across at all. The craft will not work without a spirit compounded of the salesman, the music hall performer, the parent, the clown, the intellectual, the friend, and the organizer, but the spirit will not win through on its own either. Method matters. The more 'organized' you are, the more sympathetic you can be. The better your classroom management, the more help you can be to your pupils. The highest aspirations of teaching rest upon the most mundane details of classroom management. Every word, intonation, gesture, and look counts. Furthermore, your development of your craft of the classroom allows your inner self, your personality, and your interests to benefit your pupils very deeply.

References

1. Teacher Training Agency (2002), *Qualifying to Teach, Professional Standards for Qualified Teacher Status and Requirements for Initial Teacher training*, TTA, pp. 6–12.
2. Totterdell, M., Heilbronn, R., Bubb, S., and Jones, C. (2002), *Evaluation of the Effectiveness of the Statutory Arrangements for the Induction of Newly Qualified Teachers*, DfES, Research Report 338.
3. Board of Education (1937), *Handbook of Suggestions for the consideration of teachers and others concerned in the work of public elementary schools*, HMSO, p. 124.
4. DfEE and QCA (1999), *The National Curriculum, Handbook for secondary teachers in England, Key Stages 3 and 4*, DfEE and QCA, pp. 10–42.
5. DfEE (2000), *Performance Management in Schools*, DfEE.
6. Teacher Training Agency (2002), *Qualifying to Teach, Handbook of Guidance*, TTA.
7. Teacher Training Agency (2001), Consultation Document: *Handbook to accompany the Standards for the Award of Qualified Teacher Status*, TTA, p. 7.
8. Bowlby, John (1988), *A Secure Base, Clinical Applications of Attachment Theory*, Tavistock Routledge.
9. O'Keeffe, Dennis, and Stoll, Patricia (1995), *Issues in School Attendance and Truancy*, Pitman.
10. Wheldall, K., and Merrett, F., (1989), *Positive Teaching in the Secondary School*, Paul Chapman Publishers.
11. Clarizio, Harvey F., (1971), *Towards Positive Classroom Discipline*, John Wiley and Sons.
12. Kounin, Jacob S., (1970), *Discipline and Classroom Management*, Holt, Reinhart and Winston Inc.
13. Kaplan, Avi, Gheen, Margaret, Midgley, Carol (2002), 'Classroom Goal Structure and Student Disruptive Behaviour', *British Journal of Educational Psychology*, (72).

14. James, Mary (1998), *Using Assessment for School Improvement*, Heinemann School Management Series.
15. Houghton, S., Wheldall, K., and Merrett, F., (1988), 'Classroom Behaviour Problems Which Secondary School Teachers Say They Find Most Troublesome', *British Educational Research Journal* (14).
16. Lambert, David (1999), 'Exploring the use of textbooks in Key Stage Three geography classrooms: a small-scale study', *The Curriculum Journal*, (Vol. 10, No. 1).
17. Cole, T., Crich Chinnoy, H. (1962), *Directing the Play*, Bobs-Merrill Company, New York, quoting from a talk given by Tyrone Guthrie to the Royal Society of Arts, 10 March 1952.
18. Naughton, Bill, (1967), *The Goalkeeper's Revenge and other stories*, Heinemann New Windmill Series.
19. c.f. Subsection 3 of Section 356 of the *Education Act 1996* (which repeats the *Education Reform Act 1988*), which stresses the limits of the NC requirements: 'An order ... may not require ... the allocation of any particular period or periods of time during any key stage to the teaching of any programme of study or any matter, skill or process forming part of it.'

Some helpful books

Reading about child development, aspects of schooling, and curriculum planning will continue to be interesting and stimulating throughout a teacher's career. This is not a full bibliography, but a very selective collection of books on broader aspects of schooling, which are of particular interest in terms of their implications for the craft of classroom teaching.

Brandt, Godfrey L., *The Realisation of Anti-Racist Teaching*, Falmer Press, 1986. (An aspect of every teacher's responsibilities, helpfully explored.)

Carnell, Eileen, and Lodge, Caroline, *Supporting Effective Learning*, Paul Chapman Publishing, 2002. (A very helpful book focusing on the teacherly approaches that enable the young person to understand more about how to learn effectively.)

Cooper, Hilary, Hegarty, Penny, Hegarty, Phil, and Simco, Neil, *Display in the Classroom*, David Fulton Publishers, 1996. (Although written with primary schools in mind, the practical, educative, and imaginative analysis is extremely helpful for secondary-school teachers also.)

Holmes, Elizabeth, *Newly Qualified Teachers*, second edition, The Stationery Office, 2000. (An overall guide to the requirements of 'your first years of teaching', including the statutory requirements and expanding on them.)

Imison, Tamsyn, and Taylor, Phil, *Managing ICT in the Secondary School*, Heinemann School Management, 2000. (Very useful in terms of classroom management and teaching skills involving ICT across the subject courses.)

Marland, Michael, and Rogers, Rick, *The Art of the Tutor*, David Fulton Publishers, 1997. (Covers the 'subject' of the pastoral care work of a Form Tutor, a central responsibility that virtually every secondary teacher has to take on.)

Marriott, Grace, *Observing Teachers at Work*, Heinemann School Management Series, 2001. (This covers the wider field of classroom observation, but it specifically includes sections that are especially helpful to NQTs, including the observation of their lessons and, very importantly, how they can themselves observe and gain from it.)

Shah, Monica, *Working With Parents*, Heinemann School Management Series, 2001. (Classroom management involves relating to parents, and this author covers all aspect of this important responsibility.)

Shipman, Martin, *Childhood – A Sociological Perspective*, NFER, 1972. (A sensitive and broad coverage that is helpful in thinking about the pupils in your classroom.)

Teacher Training Agency, *Qualifying to Teach, Professional Standards for Qualified Teacher Status*, TTA, 2002. (This is the revised and statutory statement of the 'Standards' required if a NQT is to have her or his qualified status confirmed at the end of the induction year. The three sections are extremely well considered and worded, and they are worth re-studying as part of Continuous Professional Development.)

Index

teachers (*cont.*)
    appraisal, 3
    attention of, getting,
        89–92
    attitudes,15–16
    caring, 6
    desk and classroom
        position, 43–4, 71–2,
        89, 92
    good, 6–9
    with groups, 93–6
    individuality, 4
    as performers, 97–118
    relationships with pupils, 6,
        8, 10–37
    role and responsibility, 1–2,
        11
    speaking, 99–104, 118
TTA Consultation Document
    2001: *Handbook to
    Accompany the Standards
    for the Award of QTS*, 11
term, preparing for, 140
threats, 30

tidiness, 39–40
time
    lessons, 119–123
    teaching career, 138–9
truancy, 55–6, 65
    registers, 63–5
videos, 87
vocabulary, 101–2

week's work, 136–8, 139–40
'withitness', 32, 71
words
    definitions, 105–6
    used to classes, 100–2
work, pupils'
    collecting, 76–7
    records, 56–60
    returning, 75–6, 77–8, 123
    storing, 74–6
work-cards and worksheets,
    79, 82–3, 128
writing in class, 128–9

year, plan, 132–3